THE DEMISE OF THE 'REASONABLE MAN'

THE DEMISE OF THE 'REASONABLE MAN'

A Cross-Cultural Study of a Legal Concept

Michael Saltman

Transaction Publishers
New Brunswick (U.S.A.) and London (U.K.)

First paperback printing 2015

This book is printed on acid-free paper that meets the American National Standard for Permanence of Paper for Printed Library Materials.

Library of Congress Catalog Number: 90-11234
ISBN: 978-0-88738-388-5 (cloth); 978-1-4128-5591-4 (paper)
Printed in the United States of America

Library of Congress Cataloging-in-Publication Data
Saltman, Michael.
The demise of the 'reasonable man' / Michael Saltman.
p. cm.
Includes bibliographical references and index.
ISBN 0-88738-388-2
1. Law - Methodology. 2. Ethnological jurispurdence. 3. Culture and law. 4. Judicial process (Primitive law) 5. Reason
I. Title.
K213.S25 1991
340'.115—dc20 90-11234
CIP

To Irit

Contents

1

Introduction

This work explores some small part of lawyers' reasonings, and because it has been written by an anthropologist, it is preconditioned by two assumptions. The first is that in almost every human society, disputes are brought before judges for resolution. And second, the process of judicial reasoning is heavily conditioned by culture, and consequently is itself a culturally relative phenomenon. This means that the present work, by disciplinary definition, is comparative and relative. Ironically, its point of departure is a claim for universalism. Gluckman has written that "the reasonable man is recognized as the central figure in all developed systems of law" (1955:83). Armed with this assertion of Gluckman, the initial aim of this project became an attempt to comparatively review the centrality, or at least the identity, of the reasonable man in both contemporary modern legal systems and in other legal cultures. For the purposes of this essay the concept of the reasonable man has been extended to incorporate any judicial pronouncement on reasonableness. Responding to a query made by the present writer to a retired judge as to if, and under what circumstances, he had ever employed the reasonable man concept in his judgments, he asserted that there are no reasonable men, only reasonable or unreasonable judges. This terse reply demanded not only a closer look at Gluckman's assertive generalization, but also some additional examination as to whether the Barotse[1] are in fact applying a reasonable man criterion for deciding their cases. It has become all too apparent that Gluckman's statement was, perhaps, more in accord with wishful thinking than a description of reality. The reasonable man plays an extremely limited role in contemporary modern legal systems, and the concept remains shrouded in its indeterminacy.

On the other hand, Gluckman's account of the Barotse legal system is convincing insofar as it demonstrates that a *form of the reasonable man concept* is being systematically applied. It provides a rationale, upon which not only is Barotse jurisprudence explicated, but which might also serve as a most appropriate framework of reference for analyzing the underlying rationales of other primitive legal systems. There are, however, both glaring contrasts as well as some undeniable similarities between the legal reasonings of Barotse judges and those of judges in our own legal system. These differences and similarities determine the broadest parameters of this study and establish the context within which relevant questions may be asked.

Couching the issue in these broadest possible terms, it is clear that similarities are indeed to be found between occurrences in both Barotse and Anglo-American courts. The obvious common denominator, albeit a functional one, is that judges in both situations are attempting to resolve disputes and provide remedies for a variety of social dysfunctions.

Eliminating from the present study what Weber has ideally described as *formal irrational* law[2], which characterizes some primitive legal cultures—trial by ordeal or the use of magical techniques—much of primitive law is, nonetheless, based on a process of reasoning. Hart has labeled this form of reasoning as "defective," "static," and "inefficient" (1961:90). On the other hand, he has not denied either the functional similarity between primitive and modern law nor that primitive law is based on any form of reasoning. But by placing primitive law outside the pale of Hart's own definition of law, and by dismissing it through the attribution of value-laden, ethnocentric labels, much useful comparative work that could serve to throw light on the workings of our own system is liable to be ignored. Employing a broad functional definition of law to the effect that all legal cultures operate on the basis of *reasoned* argument to resolve disputes between individuals and between individuals and their society, this would effectively incorporate within its scope both primitive law and its modern counterpart.

The use of the term *legal culture* is significant here. If the object of the study is the comparative analysis of legal thought processes, then the appropriate units for analysis are cultures. This would indicate that a legal system is merely one form of a legal culture based on formally systematized thought processes. The claim that such systematized thought is the exclusive criterion for determining the presence or absence of law in a society is a weak claim. Different cultures have in fact different rationales underlying the way in which they order their legal thinking. If this working definition is a valid one, then the central question of this work cuts across all legal cultures and becomes one of attempting to account for the transformation of a broad and diffuse application of the reasonable man concept in primitive society to its narrow and highly defined application in modern legal systems. While this question has its own intrinsic value, it also has obvious wider implications for theoretical questions in sociological jurisprudence and the sociology of law, as well as demanding answers to some very specific empirical questions.

The following passages, while critical of Gluckman, are not designed to detract from the central thesis that concepts of reasonableness are employed by all legal cultures. The aim is not to set up Gluckman as a "straw man," but rather to point out some of the pitfalls in making comparative assessments of what constitutes reasonableness.

Returning to the central question, Gluckman has described the difference in the application of the reasonable man concept between Barotse and modern law, as follows:

> In Barotse law "reasonableness" focuses on the extent to which persons concretely fulfil the expectations inherent in their roles as occupants of specific positions of status, while in the tests of English law and in English superior courts the "reasonable man" is much more of a judicial fiction within the differentiated realms of the law to assess fulfilment of duty within restricted dyadic relationships. (1969:19–20)

This somewhat opaque statement does little to further the argument, if all Gluckman is saying is that the reasonable man concept has limited application in modern legal systems. But in qualitative terms it is not at all clear what the difference is between the phrases, "concretely fulfil the expectations inherent in their roles as occupants of specific positions of status" and the "fulfilment of duty within restricted dyadic relationships." Both instances require the definition of standards of reasonableness for evaluating the fulfillment of either expectations or duties, and both instances also require, at the very least, a dyadic relationship that is implicit in any context of litigation. Furthermore, it is not clear why one is more of a judicial fiction than the other.

Gluckman enthusiastically applied his concept of "reasonableness" to the Barotse legal process, and the verbatim accounts of his case material make apparent sense in this context. They show that judges invariably cite standards of reasonable behavior, required by a given situation, and if either party to the dispute demonstrates in its own position a deviation from the cited norms, this enables the judges to break down that position and render a judgment. In their own reasonings, the judges concentrate, with considerable emphasis, on intention and motivation, and the litigants themselves, aware of the rules of the game, formulate their own positions in terms of reasonable or unreasonable behavior. Unlike the process of law in a modern court setting, where cross-examination is employed primarily in order to establish whether or not an act took place and where the opinions of the actors are often deemed inadmissible, there are no instances in Gluckman's cases in which opinionated evidence is ruled inadmissible.

What Gluckman may have done was to somewhat exaggeratedly overpersonalize the standards of behavior, cited in the cases, into the stereotype of the reasonable man. He was, perhaps, tempted to follow this direction, influenced by the Barotse terms, *mutu yangana*, a "man of sense" and *mutu yalakile*, an "upright man." These are stereotypes that embody the correct standards of behavior, but by his own admission he states that the judges rarely use these terms, merely implying their meanings by referring to specific statuses, for example, a "good husband," a "good fisherman," and so on (1955:126). Both in semantic and logical terms there is a substantial difference between a "man of sense" and an "upright man." The canons of justice, or criteria for decision making, will be different in either case, the man of sense being assessed by his prudence, while the upright man would, presumably, evoke recourse to moral and/or ethical standards. Even reducing the overall concept to an assessment of specific roles leaves much to be desired, since a good fisherman, judged primarily by his technical skills, is again something different from the good husband, who may be judged predominantly out of moral or ethical considerations.

Gluckman also had the tendency to rely heavily on implication and extrapolation. This emerges clearly in his 1965 article, "Reasonableness and Responsibility in the Law of Segmentary Societies," in which he replied to his critics by reevaluating their own ethnographic data in the mold of his own reasonable man model. One example of this is a case given by Gulliver from his Arusha Masai material. Gluckman inserts into the text the concepts of reasonableness and unreasonableness. Without quoting the full passage, the first two instances will provide sufficient clarification.

> A father-in-law demanded outstanding cattle from the bridewealth[3] due for his daughter, stressing that he had to have the cattle to pay tax (i.e. *he was being reasonable*). It was pointed out to the son-in-law that under Arusha custom *it is not reasonable* to expect to have a wife and children without paying cattle. (1965:145, italics mine)

This assertiveness by Gluckman is a shortcoming. In the first instance, we do not know whether the payment of tax is a reasonable cause in this particular instance for prosecuting such a claim. One could equally surmise that a prudent man would ensure the payment of his taxes on his own recognizances. Second, the obtaining of a wife and children by means of paying brideprice may have nothing whatsoever to do with reasonableness, and is simply a matter of compliance or noncompliance with Arusha Masai law. This is a clear example of an attempt by Gluckman to mold the ethnographic data of others into the concepts that he wishes to employ. His treatment of Gulliver's material is plausible, but no more than that.

Where Gluckman leaves himself open to more severe criticism is when he equates other concepts with his own ideas on the reasonable man. For example, in referring to Llewellyn and Hoebel's *The Cheyenne Way* (1941), he takes the concept of *ranges of leeway*, explained as permissible deviations from norms of behavior, and finds this to be synonymous with the reasonable man (1965:126). But as will be demonstrated, the interpretation later ascribed to this concept by the American movement of legal realism was a far cry from the meaning of the reasonable man among the Barotse.

The problem, to which Gluckman addressed himself insufficiently, is the overall rationale of the judicial process. By his own admission, the Barotse judges do not employ the abstract concept of the reasonable man when deliberating over their decisions. They are, however, citing standards of behavior that apply to people in their different roles. But it is also clear, on reading Gluckman's case material, that the standards of behavior are not *ad hoc* criteria for assessing a given situation, but rather highly idealistic and perfectionist predetermined rules. These are rules embodying expectations of what people ought to do, being tailored and applied to given situations, in most respects similar to law finding in any modern legal system. The question of reasonableness, defined in terms of purely reasoned behavior under given sets of circumstances, does not become the major issue. This may be illustrated by the modern counterpart of the test of reasonableness in *Chief Constable of Avon and Somerset v. Jones* (*Times Law Report*, 13 November 1985). The question before the appeal judges was "was it reasonable for him (the defendant) to have acted as he did, and not according to the standard of perfection yielded by hindsight?" The defendant had been driving an articulated lorry with a cargo of hay on the M-4 highway when his lights failed. He was traveling at a speed between 52 and 57 miles per hour. He immediately pulled over on the hard shoulder and collided with an unlit vehicle. The lower court, in convicting the defendant, had held that he should have braked and slowed down before turning onto the hard shoulder and should have switched on his hazard warning lights. Lord Justice Watkins, in quashing the conviction, said that the action suggested by the judge used the language of perfection. No motorist should be called upon to achieve that standard when confronted with an emergency, especially at night when his lights had failed. Justice Watkins provided the simple alternative standard: "Was it reasonable *in the circumstances* for the motorist to act as he did?" (italics mine). In this case the judges looked solely at the circumstances of the case and refused to apply any predetermined standards of behavior that are couched in perfectionist terms.

This type of reasoning is not evident in most of Gluckman's Barotse cases, since all standards of behavior have been clearly established *a priori* and are expressed in terms of preexisting moral or ethical standards. The perfectionist standard is a most convenient tool for breaking down a litigant's case. Moreover, the Barotse judges are in perhaps an even better position than their modern counterparts to determine the legislative intent of what people ought to do in given circumstances, since they are, at one and the same time, both political and judicial figures. It is they themselves who determine the standards of behavior underlying the reasonable man. This is clearly a distinctive feature of many primitive legal cultures, where there is no apparent separation of powers between the "legislature" and the judiciary, and most of the "laws" are judge-made laws. This returns the reader to one of the opening statements of this book, in which the comment of the judge quoted is echoed in Gluckman's statement that "there are therefore reasonable and unreasonable judges" (1955:153).

Reading through Gluckman's case material, it becomes extremely clear that the predetermined rules, incorporated into the reasonable man concept, are in the nature of moral and ethical imperatives. It bears out Allott's contention that in traditional society, "the area of law is entirely located within the sphere of societal morality . . . whereas in modern society there is much morality which is not expressed in law, and much law which does not correspond to any moral imperative" (1980:25). Surveying the ethnographic literature, the forms that these imperatives may assume for legal purposes are often quite varied. The closest approximation to the reasonable man, beyond a direct statement as to what a reasonable man does or should do, is the oblique reference to reasonableness as recounted in stories containing characters, real or mythological, that epitomize ideal standards of behavior in different situations. But more often than not, the usual forms are either straightforward statements of the imperative or, occasionally, its embodiment in an aphorism.

Ethical and moral imperatives are often, by nature, highly ambiguous statements that leave judges with a considerable amount of judicial latitude. By employing the reasonable man format they have an efficient technique by means of which they can mold their interpretations of current standards of morality to the facts of the given case. It is never precisely clear from Gluckman's account whether Barotse judges are asking themselves the question, if given the facts of the case, what would a reasonable man do in order to foresee the consequences of his actions. Alternatively, are they asking whether the behavior conforms to their interpretation of commonly held standards? These are very different lines of questioning, involving by definition very different forms of reasoning. The abstracted format of the reasonable, occasionally employed in the modern court setting as exemplified above by the case of the truck driver, addresses itself to nothing more than the facts of the situation, and makes no explicit *a priori* assumptions about the person's behavior. Assessment is not made on culturally loaded assumptions and thus excludes moral and ethical imperatives. This stands in stark contrast with the mode of reasoning employed by the Barotse, as reported by Gluckman.

At the other end of the continuum, at the level of the modern legal system, the reasonable man concept poses another set of difficulties. The element of foreseeability, already mentioned, has been cited by Lawson: "*[C]ulpa* amounts to failing to foresee damage, which a diligent person would have foreseen" (1950:40). Like any other adjective, "diligent" is a variable, and while not culturally biased to any great extent, is nonetheless extremely difficult to ascertain. It is perhaps easier for the judge to apply a value to this variable on the basis of hindsight, when all the facts are known. But in objective terms it is an inaccurate assessment of the actual situation, in which obviously and logically all the facts are not perceived.

Powell (1957) has written a scathing critique, attacking the semantic indeterminacy of the notion of reasonableness in the judicial process. He draws on cases to show that there are situations that do not allow for the reasoning implicit in the application of the reasonable man concept. He poses serious questions, such as whether people of subnormal intelligence, while not insane, are capable of foreseeing the consequences of their actions. He also cites a case, so patently absurd, that the standards of reasonableness applied, in order to achieve an outcome, are dubious to the extreme. In *Newberry v. Cohen's (Smoked Salmon Ltd.)*, as reported in the *Times Law Report*, 27 April 1956, the question arose as to whether "raw kippers constitute meals within the meaning of the Fifth Schedule to the Shops Act, 1950." If so, a shop could be open on Sunday to sell them. The court held, by virtue of reason, that a raw kipper could be a meal. An even more telling question is whether reasonableness is given to measurement or to mathematical tests of probability. And, finally, if the court is to use the standard of the customary or the ordinary, what is the competence of the judge to determine this standard? This last question returns to the skepticism, evoked from the outset, that there are no reasonable men, but only reasonable or unreasonable judges. Powell, in addressing himself directly to Gluckman, writes,

> Because the courts often use a phrase, which he translates by a "man of sense," he deduces that they apply the standards of the reasonable man. But most of the cases he cites show that the judges are primarily concerned with what is usual and customary, without regard to whether it is sensible and rational. (1957:119–20)

One might dispute Powell's use of the word "rational," since its supposed universality is qualified by cultural relativism (Barnes and Bloor, 1982; Overing, 1985). But it is also equally clear that the Barotse judges are not applying the Barotse equivalent of the "man on the Clapham omnibus" in order to determine what is sensible.

The words *reasonable, usual, customary, sensible,* and *rational* are bandied about as if they were, somehow, interchangeable qualities. Of these, *rational* is perhaps the most problematic category. Its usage requires a brief digression into the domain of the sociology of knowledge in order to make two points. First, the rational and the reasonable are not only nonsynonymous (rather than antonymous), but reasonableness is not necessarily to be inferred from rational postulates. Second, if certain currents of modern legal philosophy lay claim to an exclusive positivist rationality underlying a legal system, it is difficult to understand how such a system can address itself to the issues of what may or may not be reasonable. Barnes and Bloor, in holding to the relativist position, attack the so-called rationalist stand of Hollis and Lukes—who assume the existence of a universal *core* of true beliefs and rationally justified patterns of inference—when they write,

> This core is made up of statements which rational men 'cannot fail to believe in simple perceptual situations' and 'rules of coherent judgement which rational men cannot fail to subscribe to'. Elsewhere these cultural universals are described as 'material object perception beliefs' and 'simple inferences relying, say, on the laws of non-contradiction'. (1982:35)

From this Hollis and Lukes surmise that there are indeed criteria of rationality that exists independently of any given context or locally particularistic meanings.

If rationality is exemplified by the *a priori* assumption that man's mind functions universally in accordance with (yet undiscovered) neurological principles, which, for example and among other things, produce laws of non-contradiction, it can only do so in terms of meaningful perceptions. This would imply that the thought processes underlying the law of non-contradiction cannot be divorced from the context of the input of external stimuli to the mind, since the same thought processes can be activated only by that input. The input is itself context bound; therefore, it makes little difference whether the matrix for rationality exists or not. In any case, Barnes and Bloor assert that Hollis and Lukes have not demonstrated the existence of a universal core. Adopting Barnes and Bloor's claim that rationality is itself relative and context bound, it follows *a fortiori* that any judicial pronouncement on reasonableness, supposedly derived from rational considerations, is similarly relative and context bound. Moreover, there is no reason to believe that the thought processes involved in the determination of what is reasonable has anything to do with rationality from the outset. One of the questions, to which the present work has to address itself, is what major factors constitute the ingredients of the context in which judicial pronouncements on reasonableness are made.

Diamond, in reviewing Gluckman's work, also takes him to task, by demonstrating that the reasonable man has no objective standing in modern English law. He writes,

> If an English judge holds that the defendant has not used reasonable care, he means that "the defendant has not used as much care as I hold that he ought." The "reasonable man" is not the man activated by reason, or most men, or the usual or average man, but the man whom the judge takes as a standard. (1956:627–28)

The reasonable man, therefore, as a universal abstract concept, or even as a culturally relative concept, has a somewhat dubious standing. It is not clear whether judges everywhere are relying on predetermined perfectionist standards of behavior, or on the more limited consideration of what might be considered reasonable under the specific circumstances, or by some instinctive personal appraisal of what "reasonable" may mean to any particular judge.

An example of this highly "personal" approach has been provided by Lord Justice Parker in the case of *Commonwealth Smelting Ltd. and Another v. Guardian Royal Exchange Assurance Ltd.*, as reported in the *Times Law Report* on 5 December 1985. The case involved an insurance claim over the fracturing and shattering of the casing and impeller of a compressed airblower. The plaintiffs claimed that this was the result of an explosion and, therefore, was covered by the insurance policy in the event of an explosion. The defendants claimed that the accident occurred as a result of a breakage in the rotating impeller. In handing down his decision against the plaintiffs, Justice Parker stated that

> he had to ask himself whether an ordinary Englishman would say that the destruction of the blower had been caused by an explosion. He would not: he would say that it had been caused by the failure of the impeller causing a part to fly off and shatter the casing. That, not the oil pressure, had been the proximate and effective cause of the damage.

It is not clear why Lord Parker, who in this instance may have been a perfectly reasonable judge, had to find recourse in his statement to the "ordinary Englishman." It is highly doubtful that the ordinary Englishman would have assessed the technical evidence with the same degree of practiced skill exercised by Lord Parker. The citation of the ordinary or reasonable man in this instance does little to bolster the opinion of the learned judge.

The dictum that there are no reasonable men, but only reasonable judges, receives added force from Lord Macmillan's statement in *Glasgow Corporation v. Muir* (1943). While attributing some new qualities to the reasonable man, who is "presumed to be free of both over-apprehension and from over-confidence," he concedes that the standard of care, *expected* of the reasonable man, is basically subjective. But here he goes on to bear the full responsibility of the judge by saying "that it is still left to the judge to decide what, in the circumstances of the particular case, the reasonable man would have had in contemplation, and what, accordingly, the party sought to be made liable ought to have foreseen. Here there is room for diversity of view." One can only concur sympathetically with Lord Macmillan that the ultimate arbiter of what constitutes the reasonable man has to be the judge himself.

Although Powell and Diamond have rejected the test of the reasonable man as a valid legal tool, other authoritative texts have treated the concept with at least some bemused moderation. In *The Oxford Companion to Law*, the reasonable man is defined as a "hypothetical creature whose imaginary characteristics and conduct by way of foresight, care, precautions against harm, susceptibility to harm and the like, are frequently referred to as the standard for judging the actual foresight, care, etc. of a particular defendant" (Walker, 1980:1038). In this same entry, Walker goes on to describe some of the characteristics of the reasonable man concept, as cited in a number of landmark cases. But he concludes in the following vein:

> It has been observed that Lord Bramwell occasionally attributed to the reasonable man the agility of an acrobat and the foresight of a Hebrew prophet, but the reasonable man has not the courage of Achilles, the wisdom of Hercules, nor has he the prophetic vision of a clairvoyant. In truth the reasonable man is a personification of the court or jury's social judgement. There is, however, apparently no 'reasonable woman' known to common law. (1980:1038)

This last point has also been made by A. P. Herbert. In *Stroud's Judicial Dictionary* (James, 1974), the reasonable man is not even deserving of an entry. If the reasonable man, therefore, is largely a fictitious stereotype, we are still left with a large section of law that addresses itself to the concept of reasonableness, which is by no means a hypothetical issue.

Reasonable, as an adjective qualifying some other concept, lends itself more easily to the attribution of a value and its consequential use as a legal tool. In some instances it even allows for nonambiguous definition. For example, reasonable care, as defined in *The Oxford Companion to Law*, is rendered as,

> A standard of care and precaution desiderated by many rules of common law, which can be described only as being the care which a person possessed of reason would take. Such a person will guard against the obvious, the possible and the foreseeable, but not against the bare possibility, the highly unusual and the completely unexpected. He will take at least the precautions customary and normal in the circumstances. Whether care and precautions taken in a particular case measure up to reasonable care depends on the circumstances of the particular case. What is customary and normal may not be adequate and cannot be equated with reasonable care. There are some circumstances in which it would be folly to neglect certain precautions. (Ibid.)

This statement is definitive in that it categorizes the "obvious, the possible and the foreseeable" apart from "bare possibility, highly unusual and completely unexpected." But it continues into a number of opaque statements in so far as "customary and normal" is a minimal yet not necessarily an adequate requirement, and that "reasonable care" can only be assessed in terms of the peculiarities of each individual case. This is only a slight improvement over the vagueness of the original concept of the reasonable man. But at the other end of the scale one finds some very precise definitions of reasonableness. In *Stroud's Judicial Dictionary*, for example, "reasonable notice" as applied to domestic service: "Domestic service is usually terminable by a month's money or a month's notice on either side; but it may be determined at the end of the first month by a fortnight's notice on either side" (James, 1974:2268). The common law experience has defined several categories of reasonableness in varying degrees of precision (*Stroud's Judicial Dictionary* lists sixty-six of these categories).

The definitional problem of the reasonable man or reasonableness is made more complex by the different modes of reasoning required of the judges themselves. There is a significant difference in the logic of legal reasoning among the Barotse and the legal thinking of the modern judiciary. It is the primitive preoccupation with status, roles, and all the ramifications ensuing from this, that might possibly have tempted Gluckman into using the ideal stereotype of the reasonable man as a personified entity. The ultimate depersonification of legal thinking accords with Maine's position on the movement from status to contract, correlated with the emergence of the cash nexus and the transition from simple to complex society.

In simple, traditional societies, status and role differentials are sufficiently limited so as to be comprehended as a totality by both anthropologists and by the members of the society themselves. The high degree of cultural homogeneity also allows for a greater measure of shared understandings as to what constitutes the expectations of reasonable behavior. Kamenka and Tay, discussing the nature of law in *gemeinschaft*-type societies (see note 1, chap. 4), view the issue before the judiciary as that of the "whole man, bringing with him his status, his occupation and his environment, all of his history and social relationships . . . and the emphasis is on law and regulation as expressing the will, the internalized norms and traditions" (1975:136). The sheer complexity of modern society, the innumerable roles occupied by members of that society, serve to rule out shared understandings as a means for determining reasonableness.

Another factor that influences the different modes of legal reasoning relates to the basically different aims of the primitive and modern legal systems. Despite the criticism leveled against Durkheim, mainly on empirical grounds (Merton, 1965; Schwartz and Miller, 1964), there nonetheless remains some analytical value in the employment of his major categories of *restitutive* and *repressive* law. While the ethnographic data does not allow for a clear-cut association between the repressive and the primitive, and similarly between the restitutive and the modern, there still seems to be a vast preponderance of restitutive remedies in primitive society in comparison with modern society.[4] In most primitive societies we do not find a clear conceptual differentiation between criminal and civil law, clear to the extent that is such in our own society. This certainly does not mean that primitive societies treat all cases in terms of what we may understand as criminal law. Quite often it is to the contrary, the evidence indicating that under circumstances that we would be prone to define as a criminal act, the outcome in fact is that the guilty party is not punished but is required to compensate his victim. Given this major restitutive characteristic of primitive legal systems, considerable emphasis is laid on correct social behavior as a criterion for maintaining social order.

One of the guiding principles underlying this notion of correct behavior has been identified by Malinowski as that of mutuality. Malinowski constantly stressed throughout his writings that the element of mutuality provides the axiomatic basis of all social relationships and by implication, therefore, is also basic to the legal system. People abide by the law out of a sense of mutual self-interest, or for self-preservation. Mutuality provides security, and conversely, the withdrawal of mutuality serves as a sanction against an individual. Shared understanding over mutual obligations in a relatively homogeneous society, such as that of the Trobrianders, can provide a convincing and working principle for testing the concept of reasonableness. Malinowski's detractors, Radcliffe-Brown being one of the foremost, claimed that Malinowski was not really talking about law. Radcliffe-Brown adopted Roscoe Pound's position that the law constitutes "social control through the systematic application of the force of politically organized society" (1952:208). This appears to be the crux of the whole issue. It can be exemplified by the absurdly hypothetical example of Barotse and British drivers stopping at a red light. It is not at all clear whether this is the consequence of the "systematically applied force of the politically organized society," or because maybe they have a reciprocal interest together with the drivers of the traversing traffic, in so doing (out of a sense of self-preservation). In the event of an infraction, the English magistrate is little concerned with the reasonableness or unreasonableness of the accused's behavior. The law is absolutely specific on this point, and the outcome hinges on the act itself—did one stop or not stop at the red light—reasonableness, if at all a consideration, having been authoritatively predetermined by the legislature. In contrast, one could almost imagine Gluckman's hypothetical account of the

Case of the Delinquent Driver, in which the Barotse judges would soundly admonish the accused for his unreasonable behavior in not fulfilling his moral obligations as a driver.

Legal reasoning in a society in which laws are precisely formulated by a sovereign authoritative body is going to differ considerably from that in a society where this condition is absent. Precision, on the one hand, and indeterminacy, on the other, exercise their effect on the process of formulating categories. Hart has emphasized the importance of the classification of persons, things, acts, and circumstances as the essential basis for any formal legal system (1961:121). Formal legal reasoning relies heavily on analogy, and even in a modern legal system, wherein the categories have been relatively well defined, one often finds conflicting analogies, as a consequence of the use of indeterminate categories. *A fortiori* this will even further weaken the use of analogous reasoning in other legal cultures, where the categories are vague from the outset. The same difficulty is also imposed on both inductive and deductive reasoning in law. In inductive reasoning, the vaguer the categories, the more likely the increased frequency of conflicting empirical generalizations that would, by necessity, derive from the initially vague propositions. This also holds true for deductive reasoning, in which given the vaguely stated premises, the likelihood of false syllogisms emerging is considerably greater. In contemporary modern legal systems, the aim of the practitioner is to constantly whittle down indeterminacies to an essential minimum in order to apply effective logic and achieve consistency. But gaps exist in the logical construct, and it is within these gaps that the concept of reasonableness can, and does, play a role.

In order to account for the dichotomy between vagueness and precision, two important factors should be noted, one technical and the other substantive. The technical issue is simply the presence or absence of literacy. Where legal knowledge is confined solely to what may be remembered, stored, and retrieved from a man's brain, it is not only quantitatively different but is also substantively different from what is recognized as the professional reliance on textual sources. This links up with the substantive issue insofar as the "categorization of experience," a term used by Grace and Wilkinson (1978), is most conveniently achieved through normative points of reference in an individual's cognitive map. This same process of "categorization of experience," when applied to textual analysis, requires a different cognitive approach. The requirement, under these circumstances, is a cognitive appraisal of the meaning of the words in a text rather than a normative perception of the details of the act or events under consideration. In referring to the legal sources of a modern legal system, one can only concur with Grace and Wilkinson's admonition that we should "suspend the assumption that social conduct is norm-governed or motivated from shared meanings which assume a concept of a norm" (1978:260).

The reasonable man, being an indeterminable concept, lends itself to application in those areas where the law is not explicit. Stone has written that it provides by its "very vagueness and indeterminacy legal norms tolerant of conflicting situations in broad penumbral areas, even while in the core area they admit into law the more coherent insights of the society's widely shared convictions. In the former areas they cover over conflicting judgements; in the latter they promote coherence of the law with the contemporary mores" (1964:22).

A wide range of mixed feelings is espoused by modern lawyers toward the reasonable man concept, the overall attitude remaining skeptical. The essence of this skepticism is to be seen in the minority opinion given by Lord Wilberforce in *British Railway Board v. Harrington* (1972). In this opinion, he said that "to adopt the expedient of recoiling upon the comfortable concept of the reasonable man is hardly good enough. It evades the problem by throwing it into the lap of the judge." One cannot entirely sympathize with Lord Wilberforce that certain problems might have to be thrown "into the lap of the judge," particularly in those "broad penumbral areas" mentioned by Stone. Judging happens to be as much a skill as it is a science. It is certainly an evasion of the problem, if one's conceptualization of the role of the judge, in Laski's terms, is that of an "automatic slot machine into which you put a statute and from which you get a construction in which there is no articulate premise" (Robson and Watchman, 1981:40). Holmes, to whom Laski had written this last comment, maintained the more standard version of the reasonable man when he said that "the law considers, in other words, what would be blameworthy in the average man, the man of ordinary intelligence and prudence, and determines liability by that" (1881:108–9). Obviously not too satisfied with the vagueness of the concept, Holmes goes on to recommend another concept, that of *the bad man*. The bad man is a stereotype that will exploit the predictive aspect of the legal system in order to obtain material advantages in complete disregard of any moral compunction. This is Holmes' concession to the evils of formalism and admits that the law is not a hermetically sealed and closed logical system.

In fact, most lawyers bemoan the excesses of legal formalism, advocating the latitudes of reasonableness and justice, while at the same time recognizing the dominant superiority of formalism. The actual recipe for mixing these ingredients is never provided. A typical example of this is Cardozo's statement that

> the courts, then, are free in making the limits of the individual's immunities to shape their judgements in accordance with reason and justice. That does not mean that in judging the validity of statutes, they are free to substitute their own ideas of reason and justice for those of the men and women they serve. Their standard must be an objective one. (1921:89)

This quotation is quite remarkable in pointing out the anomalies of the whole situation. It provides the court with freedom beyond the boundaries of formalism, yet it rules out the judge's personal and idiosyncratic ability to apply standards of reason and justice. It assumes the consensus of reasonable attitudes of ordinary people, and that somehow all of these factors can be encapsulated within the parameters of objectivity.

Other writers have seen no impediment set by legal formalism in the law's adaptation to changing social circumstances. Levi has written,

> Legal reasoning has a logic of its own. Its structure fits it to give meaning to ambiguity and to test constantly whether the society has come to see new differences or similarities. Social theories and other changes in society will be relevant when the ambiguity has to be resolved for a particular case. (1970:104)

Levi demonstrates how reasoning by analogy can move ahead with the times without having explicit recourse to the test of reasonableness. The logical process of inclusion within and exclusion from categories allows for the influence of social theories, while it is understood that the social theories themselves do in no way determine or govern the legal theories.

But to what criteria can a judge resort? At least one of the contemporary demands on the reasonable man is that of foreseeability, but the problem remains in defining what actually is to be foreseen. As already mentioned, the assessment of the case afforded by hindsight does not necessarily accurately reflect the situation in which a person may find himself. In addition to this, there is the following problem, noted by Harari:

> it is the "reasonable man" standard of care which may refer either to what he "would" or to what he "should" foresee. The first version sanctifies existing expectations, 'reasonable' being associated with what is actually expected in the community: the second may require a standard different from such expectation, 'reasonable' being normative of what is so expected. (1962:120)

Harari's point highlights a long-standing issue of contention among legal theorists. Are the standards, employed by the courts, determined by what is occurring in everyday reality, or are they predetermined in some other way?

If the reasonable man, therefore, has relatively little application in the modern judicial scene, because it defies definition, it is perhaps appropriate that its limited application finds its most frequent expression in the domain of negligence. The specifics of the situations in which negligence can occur are myriad, so no set of equally specific sets of predetermined rules could possibly cover all contingencies. Therefore, it makes some sense that the judiciary has to fall back onto the indeterminate category of the reasonable man, from time to time, to provide cover for these situations. The characteristic of foreseeability, attributed to the reasonable man, is to be found not only in Anglo-American law, however. According to Lawson, foreseeability is coterminous with the concept of *adequacy*, as used in German, Swiss, and Scandinavian law. "A man must pay for damage of which his wrongful act is the 'adequate' cause, but for no more" (1950:62). But the actual rules, employed by the judge in determining negligence, are vague and leave much scope for the individual judge to interpret the facts of the case. Lord Samuel has posited three criteria for determining negligence in *Woods v. Duncan* (1946):

1. That the defendant failed to exercise due care.
2. That he owed the injured man the duty to exercise due care.
3. That his failure to do so was the cause of the injury.

This, of course, only partially solves the problem, since "due care" is no less wanting in definition than "reasonableness." This point often becomes painfully obvious in medical malpractice suits, where the complexities of technical evidence are often beyond the comprehension of judges. The soft underbelly of the law is, therefore, to be found in what Stone has termed the "broad penumbral areas," which remain penumbral because they defy precise, definitive categorization.

Two interim conclusions emerge at this point. The reasonable man has no concrete standing in the real world. Common to all the situations already described, and others still to be described, is the idea of the reasonable or unreasonable judge, who, in the absence of definitive rules, ascribes his own perceived notions of reasonableness to acts of behavior. Second, the judges are differentially influenced by extralegal factors. In primitive societies these usually reflect moral and ethical values, but are also tempered by political considerations, since there is no clear separation between legislative and judicial functions. In the comparative modern situation, where this separation is theoretically paramount, judges do not have the same leeway in determining reasonableness. They are constrained by precedent and legal logic and must rely solely on the delicate balance between their professional skill and their world view in order to determine what constitutes reasonableness.

In attempting to account for this transformation in the perception of the reasonable man (or reasonableness), a dominant variable to be taken into account is the shift in the locus of sovereignty from diffused to centralized political power. The consequences of this shift have had an overall effect on legal rationality (Saltman, 1985, 1987). Within the framework of this argument, the two major concepts isolated for discussion are "order" and "power." Cairns has used these two concepts in differentiating between *formal systems* and *speculative systems* of law. "The limits of the legal order in the formal systems are defined in terms of power," but for the speculative systems, "the root idea is order, not power, and the ultimate postulate is the intelligibility of the world. In a word, the speculative systems are ontological in the traditional sense" (1959: 25). If Cairns is correct, we face the following implications: Judges in primitive society, being more concerned with upholding the social order and interpreting the intelligibility of the world, are going to concentrate more on attributing meanings to social relationships than their modern counterparts.

This has been demonstrated in a paper (Saltman, 1987) comparing the development of land law in medieval England with that of changing land law among the contemporary Busoga of Uganda[5]. Both situations reflect some of the characteristics of a feudal-like social order. Disputes were originally resolved on the basis of the principles of that social order, in which the rights and obligations of the litigants were defined in terms of the statuses they occupied in relation to one another within the hierarchical structure. At a later stage of development, in both instances as a consequence of the increasing power of the centralized authority, the issues became formal ones, and claims over land rights were dependent on whether certain formal requirements had, or had not, been fulfilled. The initial situation had demanded that judicial inquiry look at the content and meaning of feudal relationships, in order to establish rights and obligations. The transformation over time, as a consequence of growing political sovereignty, ultimately emptied these relationships from their original content and redefined them solely as formal entities.

One can recognize that the reasonable man has some role to play in a legal system that is preoccupied with providing meanings to statuses and roles within a given social order. On the other hand, when rights and obligations are authoritatively defined in terms of the fulfillment or nonfulfillment of formal requirements, reasonableness has a significantly lesser role to play in the deliberations of the legal system. If judges are obliged to render decisions over issues of rights and obligations, in which the reference points are based on the cultural content of social relationships and interactions, then the stereotype of the reasonable man, in Gluckman's sense, becomes a useful tool for achieving this. Conversely, it has a limited role to play in a system wherein relationships are predominantly defined in formal terms.

The following chapters will examine the differential role of the reasonable man concept in various legal cultures and systems, and will explain the variations, primarily in relation to political factors and in particular the factor of sovereignty. In so far as it is possible, the argument will be exemplified by case material and its analysis. In addition, some attention will be paid to certain corollaries of the reasonable man concept, with special reference to the American and Scandinavian schools of legal realism. While the title of this book is *The Demise of the Reasonable Man*, there is no reason why he should not be resurrected in one form or another in the future.

Notes

1. The Barotse form a group of tribes making up a kingdom in the western region of Zambia (formerly Northern Rhodesia). The dominant tribe within this group is the Lozi, and the terms *Lozi* and *Barotse* are used interchangeably by Gluckman. The traditional economy was based on horticulture, animal husbandry, and fishing. The Lozi also maintained extensive trading relations with neighboring tribes. Above the nuclear family level the village is the basic territorial and organizational unit for economic, political, and domestic activities. Land is held "in title" by the village headman and is allocated to the villagers who reside in the territory of that headman. Villages are organized into larger political entities that were associated, in the past, with two regional capitals—the northern ruled by the king, and the southern ruled by a chief subordinate to the king. The British divided the territory into a number of administrative districts, linked to two new provincial capitals. Between the village level and the highest office of the kingdom, there was an ascending hierarchy of political functionaries engaged in the raising of tribute and its redistribution, in addition to which it also performed judicial functions. A more detailed account of the operation of the legal system is supplied in note 2, chapter 2. Lozi religion combines both pagan and Christian elements.
2. Weber employs four major ideal-type categories of legal thought. Having eliminated the *formal irrational* for consideration in this text, the remaining three categories are subject, in one way or another, to the relevancy of reasonableness. The *substantive irrational*, unguided by

general principles or rules, addresses itself to each individual case as a separate issue and treats it on its own merits. Such an approach is liable to rely heavily on *ad hoc* concepts of reasonableness. The *substantive rational* rests on the principles of a given ideological system—political, economic, ethical, or religious—which expresses, at the very least, a conceptualization of reasonableness, albeit in ideal terms. Finally, even if the *formal rational* assumes a logical basis to its form of reasoning, the ensuing system of thought is not "gapless," and the indeterminacies often require the judiciary to deal with the question of what may or may not be reasonable.

3. Bridewealth is sometimes mistakenly understood as the outright "purchase" of a wife. The correct perspective for viewing this institution is one of compensation to the bride's family for the woman's detachment from her own group after marriage and the transferral of her reproductive capacity to the benefit of another group. The payment of bridewealth legalizes the status of children born from the marriage. The payment of bridewealth is seen as an important legal obligation in many non-Western societies.
4. This argues against Durkheim's original thesis that in primitive society the violations of the collective conscience are dealt with by repressive measures (i.e., punishment). Conversely, Durkheim viewed modern society very much in terms of the restitution of balances for the purpose of maintaining social solidarity, and, accordingly, the law is designed for its restitutive effect. What Durkheim apparently ignored is the fact that in many primitive societies there is no adequate political mechanism that can effectively apply the coercive sanctions characterizing repressive law. In the absence of such mechanisms, there is a corresponding reliance on restitutive law.
5. The Busoga tribe is one of the Interlacustrine Bantu kingdoms of East Africa. The Soga territory is bounded by Lake Victoria to the south, Lake Kyoga to the north, and the Nile to the west. The Soga engaged in the cultivation of millet, plantain, sweet potato, and maize, in addition to which they also maintained livestock. Above the level of the nuclear family the Soga are organized in localized corporate lineages. These patrilineages are reinforced by a religious ideology, based predominantly on ancestor worship. The political structure of the Soga is described in some detail in chapter 2.

2

Norms as a Function of the Judicial Process: The Ethnographic Data

One of the findings of the previous chapter is that in the absence of explicitly stated rules, judges may have to fall back on the relatively indeterminate category of reasonableness in order to achieve a resolution of the case. This occurs in relatively low frequency within our own legal system, which strives ideally to be a "gapless" system yielding a high level of predictability for its outcomes. A modern legal culture, in comparison with many of its primitive counterparts, is a system and, as such, lays claim to a scientific rationale. Correspondingly, primitive legal cultures do not exhibit these features and rely heavily on reasonableness as a practical tool for achieving the resolution of disputes. In both instances, reasonableness is strongly associated with normative and customary behavior, which remain in the form of very broad parameters of reference in noncomplex legal cultures, but are constantly being subjected to definition, as demanded by the modern system. Furthermore, the normative element has been somewhat watered down in the modern context. In contemporary Anglo-American law the normative is implicitly incorporated within the rule as a component of the legislative process. Hart has described the criteria that accord validity to laws—a primary rule of obligation and a secondary rule of recognition (1961:79–88). In practice, the latter sometimes outweighs the former in its significance, for the maintenance of the system (by means of the secondary rules of recognition) is no less important a consideration than the outcome of any given case. It is the authoritative statement of the rule that ultimately controls or directs the judge rather than the judge having to search for the meaning of the primary rule of obligation or to examine the meaning of the behavior he is being required to judge.

If, as a general rule, the explicitly stated and authoritatively defined rules minimize the need to search for meanings in terms of the normative facets of reasonableness, it is nonetheless precisely within the judicial process that we find the definition of norms. Social scientists have the tendency to talk and write glibly about norms, as if they constitute well-defined entities rather than as something belonging to the existential. Anthropologists, perhaps more than others, seem to assume that norms will reveal themselves through the methodology of participant-observation. But the determination of norms, particularly in an alien culture, cannot be the simple outcome of observing and recording recurrent behavior patterns, this often being the way norms are represented in anthropological research. The assumption that norms may be inferred from Durkheimean "social facts" is misleading. There is something more to a norm than a mere statistical expression of recurrent items of social behavior. The delineation of norms also requires a statement of the additional dimension of the actors' perceptions of their own behavior patterns, since norms also constitute *perceived* representations of meaningful behavior. It is assumed more often than not that because people are not consciously aware of the norms that motivate their everyday behavior, they are not attributing meaning to them. At one level, norms are meaningful insofar as they provide individuals with cognitive points of reference that enable them to interact correctly with other people in an infinite number of situations, irrespective of whether the situation and the people involved are familiar or unfamiliar. It is at this juncture that the concepts of norms and reasonableness link up, since the norms provide reasonable expectations of how people will interact in given situations. This is, perhaps, the most basic feature of reasonableness.

At another level, norms are enunciated, ascribed meanings, and given to interpretation. This is the level of the judicial process. It is the suspected breach of a norm that brings people to the state of conscious consideration of its meaning. This is especially true in primitive societies; in contemporary modern society it is more often the rule that is being breached rather than the norm that underlies that rule.

In the judicial deliberations of primitive societies, and in the aftermath of public comment on these deliberations, we may learn what is the norm in question. But, perhaps of greater importance is the fact that we may also learn what are the permissible leeways of behavior on either side of the norm. These leeways are not discernable in the usual fieldwork procedure of recording regularities in behavior, which are then presented as the representative norms. One might legitimately take anthropologists to task for paying insufficient attention to the judicial process in the societies they study, in addition to the specifics of the actual topic they are studying. The judicial process cuts across all aspects of societal life and provides significant insights as to how people conceptualize their own normative behavior in all domains. It is certainly one of the more authoritative emic* statements about people's behavior. By the same token, one can also criticize those anthropologists who do study the anthropology of law for not having sufficiently emphasized the wider methodological benefits accruing from the study of the legal process.

Nadel, a particularly insightful anthropologist, cautiously reflects some of this thinking. He states,

> Nor does "reasonable" stand only for adherence to custom but also for the permissible latitude or "leeway" in that adherence, with which every society must reckon, as it were, naturally and within reason. In this sense the stipulated reasonableness would seem to bear on the character of men and societies everywhere, over and above the subspecies of "Lozi Man." (1956:166)

The treatment of the enthnographic data in this chapter will be based on the contrasted uses of two models of reasonableness. The

**Emic*, deriving from the word phonemic, is a description of meaningful cultural categories as held by a particular cultural group. This stands in contrast to *etic*, deriving from the word phonetic, which is a description of cultural categories as generalized phenomena that are both objectively verifiable and valid as categories for the purpose of cross-cultural comparison.

first approach is the Gluckman stereotypic version of the reasonable man, who represents the sterling virtues of conformity with custom, moral uprightness, and prudence. This is relatively overt and straightforward. The standards employed are commonly shared understandings that are openly evoked as abstract statements, usually in the form of moral and ethical imperatives. These constitute the standards for determining only one level of reasonableness. But it is, perhaps, too rigid a criterion for establishing reasonableness, since it sets ideally high standards of behavior as a measure, to which most people in real life do not, and probably cannot, totally conform. This point obtains some credence insofar as in the typical Barotse case, more often than not, all the parties to the case are soundly rebuked by the judges. In at least one case, the judge is accused of the same failing for which he himself, in another case, had chastised another litigant on moral grounds.

The other approach, initially set out by Llewellyn and Hoebel (1941), and later developed by the former into his concept of the "Grand Style" of judging (1960), is, perhaps, more difficult to comprehend. They associate norms with what they term *felt standards for proper behavior*. "It is, moreover, the felt norms for conduct, which are likely to be injected into the case of breach. Per contra, it is the case of the hitch or trouble that dramatizes a 'norm' or a conflict of 'norms' which may have been latent. It forces conscious attention: it forces the defining of issues" (1941: 21). The second point of importance that Llewellyn and Hoebel emphasize is the two *ranges of leeway* of man's conduct, which are part of any legal or social system—"the range of the permissible and the range of the actively protected leeway" (1941:23). The notion of leeways more accurately characterizes ideas of reasonableness than the positing of high moral and ethical standards of behavior. In some of Gluckman's cases these latter standards, occasionally and paradoxically, appear to be highly unreasonable because of their rigidity and perfectionism. Llewellyn and Hoebel repeatedly note the inability of their Cheyenne[1] informants to address themselves either to hypothetical issues or to provide any coherent statements about their norms in an abstract form. This raises the question as to whether reasonableness is a product of consciously predetermined and enunciated standards of an almost precedentlike quality, or whether it is merely an *ad hoc* assessment of behavior, based on the personal knowledge and intuitions of the judges. Without begging the question, it is most likely that the answer is a subtle combination of these two forms.

In order to illustrate this fundamental difference in attitudes toward reasonableness, the one based on the shared understanding of "felt norms," the other based on abstract statements of moral and ethical imperatives, the differential Barotse and Cheyenne treatment of sexual transgressions will be considered. The ethnographic purist may raise some strong objections as to the reliability of Llewellyn and Hoebel's field data. The cases are all reconstructions elicited from informants. But the accuracy of the specific details have little bearing on the overall principles being considered here. There appears to be remarkable consistency throughout all their case material that serves to lend considerable credence to the presence of the so-called felt norms in Cheyenne society. It is this phenomenon that is relevant to the present study.

Llewellyn and Hoebel claim that adultery was rare among the Cheyenne, but when a husband was, in fact, cuckolded, his best reaction was to ignore it. "They (the Cheyenne) had a phrase for it—'a dog has pissed on my tent'" (1941:189). The case of Shoots-Left-Handed (1941:187–89) adequately demonstrates the Cheyenne notion of reasonableness in this respect.

Shoots-Left-Handed returned from a prolonged war expedition to find his wife pregnant. On questioning his wife as to who was responsible, she told him that it was his friend Sharp-Eyes. Shoots-Left-Handed brought the matter before the Society of the Elk Soldiery. While this was going on, Sharp-Eyes' father, on his own initiative, sent a gift of horses to Shoots-Left-Handed, and at the same time sent Sharp-Eyes back to the Elk Lodge, from which he had in the meantime been ostracized. When the horses, sent by Sharp-Eyes' father, were delivered to the lodge, Shoots-Left-Handed refused to smoke the pipe until his fellow soldiers rendered their verdict, which he regarded as binding. Sharp-Eyes was called to the lodge, given a pipe to smoke and was asked if he was guilty or not. He admitted to his guilt and immediately offered to compensate Shoots-Left-Handed by providing material support for the child after its birth. The assembled soldiers intimated to Shoots-Left-Handed that he should accept this offer, which he did.

A Barotse case, based on similar circumstances, provides a completely different remedy. Gluckman obtained this case from a text (uncited) and it is recounted in full here (1955:191). A man was away working in White Country for some years. When he returned home, his father met him and told him that his wife had a child by a well-known ne'er-do-well and begged him not to beat her. The father considered that the son had driven his wife to wrongdoing by his long absence and that she was nevertheless a good wife. The son accepted these admonitions and agreed to retain his wife unreproved and to accept the adulterine child. The *kuta*[2] at Liluai upheld his suit for damages against the adulterer but refused to countenance his plea, against the adulterer's father, that he keep the child. The *kuta* admitted that the adulterer was too much of a wastrel to pay the damages or to care for the child as well as the offended husband would, but held, "It is hard, but is the law: a child must go to its father." A short account of another Barotse case serves to throw some additional light on Barotse attitudes to reasonableness. In Gluckman's Case of the Adulterer's Good Husband, a man who continued to care for his wife and her parents after he decided to divorce her for getting a child in adultery, was highly commended by the *kuta* for being a proper upright man" (1955:134–44).

The juxtaposition of these cases indicates a number of clear contrasts. The outcome of the Cheyenne case reveals the linkage between its apparently reasonable outcome and the felt norms of the participants. The emotional animosity that usually accompanies adultery cases is conspicuously absent, or at the very least extremely well concealed, in the account of this case. A clue, throwing some light on this factor, is in Llewellyn and Hoebel's description of men's attitudes toward women in the event that the latter abscond. [I]t did not fit a Cheyenne warrior's ideal conception of dignity to chase a woman who did not want him . . . consequently husbands usually gave little external evidence of emotional tension when wives sought new spouses" (1941:190).

The actual act of adultery was not the overt issue in the Cheyenne case, particularly since Sharp-Eyes had already been sanctioned by public opinion by being ostracized from the Elk Lodge. The series of events that actually took place were all self-remedying acts, with almost no formal directives from the judicial body, designated in this case as the soldiery of the Elk Lodge. Sharp-Eyes's father had already sent horses as compensation for the act of adultery, Shoots-Left-Handed had made it clear from the outset that he would abide by any decision, and Sharp-Eyes had volunteered to provide material assistance for the child. In clear distinction to the Barotse example, the matter of the legal rights over the child is totally ignored. Even the final Cheyenne decision was rendered as a recommendation rather than as a prescription. It contained no moralizing, no enunciation of condemnation, not even apportionment of blame. The canons of reasonableness are based, in large measure, on rigid self-control and clearly shared understandings about expected behavior. Included within this reasoning was also the consideration of the benefit of the yet-unborn child, this contrasting strongly with the Barotse outcome.

On reading the Cheyenne case prior to the Barotse one, it may have the effect of skewing the impression made by the Barotse example toward its lack of reasonableness, specifically the statement "it is hard, but is the law." For in this phrase there are the seeds of an implicit recognition of the unreasonableness of the situation. But it is hardly the case that the Barotse are being totally unreasonable. They seem to fully realize that the handing over of the child to its "wastrel" biological father is a bad thing. But in terms of priorities, and even more important, in terms of principles, reasonableness means that children belong to their fathers. There are too many complex social factors at stake in this matter to confine the definition of reasonableness solely to the terms of the specific case.

Structurally, the Barotse are a more complex society than the Cheyenne. They are apparently aware of the implications that their decision making has for the "system" as a whole. The consideration for what may be construed as the public interest, as expressed by the system, probably outweighs the specifics of the individual case. The fact that children belong to their fathers relates to all kinds of extraneous factors, such as bridewealth, the economic and political value of children, as well as the question of the inheritance of property. The only item of "felt" norms, defining reasonableness in Gluckman's account of the case, is the son's recognition of his father's admonition that his prolonged absence may have been the cause of his wife's adultery. Even in going against their "felt" norms, the Barotse judges assume a customary norm of reasonableness in order to justify their decision—"a child must go to its father." This is the authoritative statement of accepted custom, made by the formally constituted judicial body of the Barotse. This body is made up of functionaries drawn from the various levels of the political hierarchy. This close relationship between politics and law in the Barotse context often seems to give rise to paternalistic expressions of reasonableness, as exemplified by the second Barotse case, wherein the husband is commended as a "proper upright man."

Ethnographers of law have, on the whole, ignored the entire domain of public reaction to judicial decisions. Little effort has been made to obtain comments, interpretations, and analyses from the native observers of the judicial events. Examination of these attitudes would probably reveal prevailing attitudes toward reasonableness in the judicial process. One has to assume that there was some public discussion over the Barotse decision to hand over the child to its incompetent biological father, and this discussion might have indicated whether or not the judge's version of reasonableness (i.e., that "a child must go to its father") conformed with public opinion. Certainly any discussion on the dilemma posed by the conflicting versions of reasonableness would have been instructive in this case. Similarly, we shall never know from the second example whether "the proper upright man" was widely regarded as such, or whether others might not have regarded him as a fool. Public attitudes toward reasonableness appear to play an important role among the Cheyenne, and seem to operate most clearly at the fringes of the legal system. This attitude is replicated in some measure in Malinowski's account of Trobriand law[3]. The following cases will illustrate this point.

Llewellyn and Hoebel describe a sequence of events following the elopement of Red Owl's daughter (1941:160–61). Red Owl, who from all accounts appeared to be a thoroughly obnoxious woman, scolded and whipped her daughter after she had eloped. Red Owl's sons left the tipi in disgust at her actions, shortly to be followed by Red Owl herself. The daughter, remaining in the tipi, committed suicide by shooting herself. The immediate ensuing public reaction was one of outrage, and everyone present, including one of Red Owl's sons, began to beat her severely. She was saved from certain death at the hands of the crowd only by the timely intervention of her sister. Red Owl, thereafter, was totally ostracized and banished from the community, although it is interesting to note that after the lapse of a considerable period of time, she was allowed to rejoin the community on a somewhat limited basis. This was not an isolated case. Llewellyn and Hoebel provide an additional example of a girl who had left her husband, was similarly berated by her mother, and as a consequence, hanged herself. The women of the camp threatened the mother's life, and she was in fact beaten by her husband, after which she fled from the camp.

The case for comparative purposes, given by Malinowski, is one of the classical cases to be found in the literature on the anthropology of law—the case of Kima'i:

> The boy had committed suicide. The truth was that he had broken the rule of exogamy, the partner in his crime being his maternal cousin. . . . This had been known and generally disapproved of, but nothing was done until the girl's discarded lover . . . took the initiative. This rival . . . insulted the culprit in public, accusing him in the hearing of the whole community of incest and hurling at him certain expressions intolerable to a native. For this there was only one remedy . . . he (Kima'i) climbed a coco-nut palm, and addressed the community . . . bidding them farewell. He explained the reasons for his desperate deed and also launched forth a veiled accusation against the man who had driven him to his death, upon which it became the duty of his clansmen to avenge him. Then he wailed aloud, as is the custom, jumped from the palm some sixty feet high and was killed on the spot. There followed a fight within the village in which the rival was wounded; and the quarrel was repeated during the funeral. (1926:78)

These cases illustrate a number of interesting facets to the concept of reasonableness. Both the Cheyenne and the Trobriand instances were initially instigated by the breaking of a rule. Llewellyn and Hoebel concentrate more on the act of suicide itself than on the initial infringement of the rule. For them, "Cheyenne suicide as a legal, or better, extra-legal proceeding, involved more than shame or grief or weariness or glory: it was an appeal, direct and extreme, to justice beyond the law—and so, in its groping way, for better law" (1941:165). They bring little evidence to support this assertion, which appears to be more the wishful thinking of Llewellyn throughout his professional career—the groping for better law.

Malinowski's analysis, on the other hand, is more sophisticated insofar as he links the act of initial lawbreaking with its tragic outcome. An illicit sexual relationship with a classificatory sister (the maternal cousin) is a gross breach of the exogamy rule. This, of course, is the ideal norm, upheld by universal consensus. Similarly, the ideal norm for women's behavior among the Cheyenne has been stated by Grinnell: "The women of the Cheyenne are famous among all the western tribes for their chastity" (1915:156). Furthermore, it was the women of the tribe, according to Llewellyn and Hoebel, who traditionally inflicted the sanctions in the event of a breach of chastity (1941:177). But in both the Cheyenne and Trobriand cases, the formal statement of the rule is an expression of the ideal rather than the real, since the facts of real life apparently deviate considerably from the ideal norm, particularly in sexual matters. Of the fifty-four cases cited by Llewellyn and Hoebel, sixteen involved, in one way or another, the sexual delicts of women, obviously aided and abetted by men. Malinowski, in pointing out "that the natives show horror at the idea of violating the rules of exogamy," goes on to state that "I found the breach of exogamy—as regards intercourse and not marriage—is by no means a rare occurrence" (1926:79–80).

Malinowski's account of the Trobriand practice is somewhat marred by a value judgment, in which he accuses the Trobrianders of hypocrisy (1926:80). Maybe they are hypocritical on this issue, but that is not particularly relevant to the study of the legal phenomena involved. Sexual promiscuity is very much a fact of life in all societies at all times, and attitudes toward it, while tending to be ambiguous, are nonetheless significantly patterned. The Trobrianders, aware of its presence, are tolerant as long the behavior is discrete, but when the act is blatantly brought to the attention of the community, the ideal is activated and the culprits have to pay the penalty. But the community is no less outraged at the individual who publicly disclosed the indiscretion, and in both the Cheyenne and Trobriand examples, these individuals were severely beaten with full public approval. In these instances, reasonableness and unreasonableness at the margins of the issue are being debated in terms of felt norms and ideal norms.

What Malinowski, Llewellyn, and Hoebel seemed to have missed is the discussion of the leeways that bridge the gap of reasonableness between the formally stated ideal norm and the felt norms that reflect public opinion. It is really these leeways that constitute the parameters of the reasonable man in the legal process, and not necessarily the strict adherence to the ideal. Malinowski correctly stated that in "moral matters it is easy and pleasant strictly to adhere to the ideal—when judging the conduct of others or expressing an opinion about conduct in general" (1926: 79). This reflects in large measure the reasonings of Barotse judges, and there is probably far less of the reasonable man in the Barotse legal process than Gluckman had assumed. Alternatively, we may have to admit the possibility of the ascription of different meanings to the concept of the reasonable man.

The assumption of variable norms of reasonableness is, in part, a function of varying degrees of political sovereignty in different societies. An explanation cannot be so simplistic as to assume that Trobrianders and Cheyenne were more tolerant, or more reasonable than others, because they have a certain kind of *ethos*. It is even dubious to assume that they are, in fact, tolerant. Leeways exist when the customary law is not explicit, when the authorities are not sufficiently powerful to enforce adherence to the rules, or where there is a strong ideological, but not necessarily doctrinaire, commitment to a given way of life. But as already stated, leeways are merely one form of assessing reasonableness. As authority becomes more centralized and powerful, the tendency is toward more official and explicit versions of what constitutes reasonableness. Furthermore, as legal thinking gravitates toward the mode of logical positivism, there is correspondingly less recourse toward finding meanings for behavior, and reasonableness, as a concept, becomes in itself meaningful and relevant only when the logical imperfections of the system militate against the provision of a remedy.

Reasonableness is identifiable when judges are searching for meanings in patterns of behavior. The progressive development of legal thought has transformed what were, in the past, meaningful relationships within a given social order, into strictly formal sets of relationships, as defined by the law. This process has been described (Saltman, 1987), and is summarized as follows.

A comparison of land law, between what obtained in twelfth- and thirteenth-century England and what occurred in the recent history of the Busoga of Uganda, reveals a number of common features. The general social structure in both instances is based on an ideal feudal concept[4] of social order, wherein political and economic links are forged on the basis of personal bonds of loyalty of an inferior toward a superior, in an ascending hierarchy of rulers to the apex of a paramount ruler. The social order, at its lowest levels, rested on shared understandings about mutual rights and obligations, and in the event of disputes, judges would effectively interpret the social order. A basic factor here is that in both cases rulers rule over people rather than over a territory, a point constantly stressed by Fallers (1969) with reference to the Busoga. And by the same token, the feudal monarch in England was *Rex Anglorum* and not *Rex Anglie*. If the shared understandings about mutual obligations in the feudal order provided the legal rationale whereby the resolution of disputes was achieved through the courts' interpretations of the meanings of that order, this inevitably had to change as a consequence of changing socioeconomic and political conditions.

The lifetime feudal relationship between a subject and his ruler was pitted against the principle of heredity, which supposedly guaranteed rights of succession on equal terms. This principle, in turn, was pitted against the reversionary rights of rulers, who wished to evict tenants for pecuniary gain. In addition, the growing tendency toward a cash nexus, as a substitute for the actual performance of mutual rights and obligations, had a considerable effect in depersonalizing social relationships. But the cash nexus also provided the profit motive for the ruler to dispossess his tenant, and toward the end of the twelfth century in England, rulers were asserting their reversionary rights, against the principle of heredity, at a significantly accelerated rate. Milsom, in describing this situation, states that "the mischief originally aimed at was, therefore, not a disorder of which wrongdoers might take advantage, but an order in which lords might abuse their customary powers of control" (1981:135). In Uganda the same type of abuse of reversionary rights also occurred. Chiefs and headmen, who had formerly subsisted from tax farming, had now become low-salaried civil service functionaries (Fallers, 1956). One effective way of increasing income under these circumstances was to evict tenants, reallocate the land, and collect substantial entry fees from the new tenants. It is not surprising, therefore, that litigation over land disputes rose sharply both in twelfth-century England and in Uganda. But in order to understand the response of the legal system to this new situation, one has to look at the political context, wherein, once again, a common denominator in both English and Ugandan examples becomes apparent.

A political battle over sovereignty was being fought. In England the king was attempting to establish his own centralized powers at the expense of his feudal lords, while in Uganda the British colonial Local African Government aspired to more than nominal sovereignty by reducing the traditional powers of chiefs and headmen. The development of royal courts in England and the colonial government courts in Uganda, as an alternative form of access to justice, played a crucial role in the battle over sovereignty. But it also had a profound effect on the rationality underlying legal decision making.

What emerges in both situations is a rationale that at one and the same time maintains continuity with past historical realities but uses a different kind of logic to achieve remedies. Fallers has described this for the Busoga by claiming that the sovereign source of power to allot headmanships and associated tracts of land had become a mere historic source of rights. What had formerly constituted political powers had now become a legal concept denoting powers no longer exercisable, and the legal concept in this form became subject to interpretation by the courts (1969:244). The courts' interpretation becomes that of analyzing property rights rather than that of searching for the meanings of social relationships. In this context the reasonable man has little or no role to play. Insofar as the comparable English situation is concerned, the very same phenomenon becomes evident. Milsom has written that "litigants preferred to go directly to the king's court and its rules became rules about abstract property rights in which lords played no part. Seisin becomes like possession, a relation between one person and a piece of land; and the lord, the second person in the original idea vanishes" (1981:124). A new logic was now imposed by the higher courts, the enabling factor, in part, being the sanctions that could be imposed by the central government. The court was obliged to provide an affirmative or negative answer to questions that were based on an exclusively formal issue. Both in England and in Uganda the question was whether the claimant had met all the necessary formal requirements for obtaining his initial rights to the land. This principle was established by the Assize of Mort d'ancestor in 1166 in England, and in what could be construed as a landmark case, cited by Fallers (1969:274–75) for the Busoga: *Asumani v. Musa*.

The case of Asumani considers the criteria for abandonment as grounds for the headman to exercise his reversionary right. Asumani claimed that he was unjustifiably dispossessed of his land by the subvillage chief, Musa. The original allotment had been made by the village headman, Sowobi, but in 1938 Asumani moved his family into another subvillage and received a plot there, but nonetheless continued to cultivate his original allotment. Asumani's contention was that his continued cultivation of the disputed plot indicated nonabandonment, while the cultivation of the second plot in his new abode was a consequence of the low economic yield of the original plot. Musa's argument was based on the past historical reality that the allotment of a piece of land implies a personal relationship of allegiance between a man and his ruler. Therefore, the act of leaving the subvillage and living in another subvillage was tantamount to abandonment. Note that the arguments of both litigants are couched in terms of expected standards of reasonableness. Asumani is claiming economic exigency as a reasonable leeway, while Musa lays claim to what he expects should be reasonable behavior, in its customary sense, from his politically subordinate and dependent tenant. The court, in its decision, ignored both these arguments and found in favor of Asumani in the following terms: "The holding which he claims from Musa is his. It was allotted to him by Sowobi." Thus, the land was not subject to reversionary right. From this it may be concluded that the formal act of the initial allotment constituted the test for the court in determining the legal status of the plot as long as the land was being actively cultivated.

The issue remains one of rights in holdings deriving from the initial allotment, and the question of allegiance to a ruler becomes irrelevant. Similarly, the writ of Mort d'ancestor (Hall, 1965:150) requires jurors to provide affirmative or negative answers to three formal questions: Was the father of the plaintiff in legal possession of the land? Did he die after a given date? Is the plaintiff his legal heir? If all the answers are in the affirmative, the plaintiff recovers his land. In both instances, (Mort d'ancestor and the Ugandan court decision) the outcome is based on the examination of a set of formal conditions rather than an interpretation of the meaning of social relationships. If the formal requirements were met, the claimant would be put in possession. Any other questions appertaining to the patterns of behavior between the litigants and, consequently, any appeals to the standard of the reasonable man become totally irrelevant in this kind of decision-making process.

To sum up to this point, the linkage between reasonableness and sovereignty is clearly an important factor. The validity accorded to standards of reasonable behavior by the judicial process appears to pass through some roughly defined phases, which are themselves linked to varying degrees of increasing sovereignty. The relatively egalitarian societies, represented so far by the Cheyenne and the Trobrianders, have a shared but indeterminate set of perceptions regarding what constitutes proper and reasonable behavior. These are rarely evoked as conscious principles in an abstract sense, and Llewellyn and Hoebel have taken pains to point out that the Cheyenne are incapable of addressing themselves to hypothetical issues or abstract legal principles. Even though the Cheyenne and Trobriand islanders have chiefs, these leaders have no formally constituted authority to apply coercive sanctions. Prior to European intervention, crimes committed against the person of a chief among the Trobrianders were punishable by death. But in most egalitarian societies, sanctions are, more often than not, supernatural. Malinowski points out that Trobriand chiefs have to hire sorcerers, at their own expense, in order to apply this sanction (1926:92).

Malinowski stated quite categorically that norms of obligation are grounded in mutuality and reciprocity, and that as a consequence, deviants would have their rights withdrawn from them. This comes in place of punitive sanctions, and is certainly borne out by the evidence from both the Trobrianders and the Cheyenne. But Malinowski goes somewhat astray in his enthusiasm for this point by stating, "Taking our stand upon such a comprehensive view of law and inquiring into the nature of the forces which make it obligatory, we shall be able to arrive at much more satisfactory results than if we were to discuss questions of authority, government and punishment" (1926:13). There is, of course, a glaring error in this statement of Malinowski, since questions of authority, government, and punishment are, in many societies, integral to the forces that make law obligatory in those societies. While undoubtedly making a significant contribution in demonstrating the potent forces of mutuality and reciprocity, he erred by placing almost exclusive weight on it.

The conditions established by colonialism provide an almost controlled comparative context, within which law underwent an accelerated development, paralleling some facets of the long-term development of Anglo-American and Continental legal systems over centuries. The relationship between the colonial authorities and the indigenous customary law was very much like that of a marriage of convenience. In particular, the British relied heavily on customary law, as part of the policy of indirect rule, in order to provide remedies for civil disputes between native litigants. But the real locus of power rested with the colonial authorities, a degree of power and sovereignty previously unknown in those territories. This ultimately had to have its effect on the rationale of customary law, now operating under totally different political and economic conditions. Customary law in the colonial situation functioned merely as a "semi-autonomous field," in Moore's terms (1978), since full sovereignty now rested in the wider legal setting of the colonial authorities. The effects have been well summarized by Chanock, who in commenting on MacGaffey's work in the Congo, writes that "custom was transformed from a way of representing and manipulating the world into a set of government rules" (1985: 47). Similarly, MacGaffey states that "under indirect rule, the indigenous code of symbolism, rhetoric and magic was made to serve an administrative code subject to judicial enforcement" (1970:303).

Unfortunately, MacGaffey does not provide sufficiently detailed case material. But the same process of transformation has been noted by the present writer in the case of the Kipsigis[5], a Kalenjin-speaking group in southwestern Kenya (Saltman, 1977). The Kipsigis had their own concepts of reasonableness, governed mainly by the fact that their indigenous judicial bodies could not impose coercive sanctions in what may be termed *civil disputes*. This resulted in a closing formula at the end of each case, in which both parties were asked to confirm their assent to the decision, and if not, the judicial body convened again, and as many times as was necessary, for achieving a remedy that was acceptable to all parties. Under these circumstances, it is clear that the aim of the judiciary was to appeal to the litigants' sense of reason in order to achieve some sort of a compromise. Sometimes these cases continued over an extended period of several sessions, and occasionally a remedy was never found. But unlike the Barotse, the appeal to reasonableness among the Kipsigis was not normally made on a high moral or ethical level, but was based rather on pragmatic and commonsensical considerations.

This last point is illustrated by two cases, the one taken from the Kipsigis material and the other from the Tiv[6], as reported by Bohannan (1957:103–4). The circumstances of both these cases are approximately similar. The Kipsigis case is as follows. The plaintiff bought a calf from the defendant. Since his grazing plot was not as yet ready, he asked the defendant to carry on looking after the calf. When he came to see his calf a few months later, he was informed by the defendant that it had died. The defendant claimed that he had shown the carcass to the plaintiff. The presentation of evidence and the cross-examination of witnesses indicated that in all probability the calf had been spirited away by the defendant and that the carcass shown was not that of the calf. But the decision was not rendered on this basis, even though it was widely assumed that the defendant was lying. The Kipsigis have an institutionalized system of cattle lending that cross-cuts the whole society, establishing a wide network of social relationships as well as providing a sort of insurance policy against cattle disease hitting a particular area. In the event of a loaned head of cattle dying, the borrower has to immediately inform the lender and return the skin as proof. While the present case was not strictly an example of cattle lending, the judges extended the provisions of the principle to cover this case, and since the defendant had not informed the plaintiff, he was found liable. The defendant rightly claimed that this had not been the arrangement, yet nonetheless agreed to the verdict. The defendant knew only too well that the public knowledge of what had happened was widespread, and accepted the reasonableness of the decision, first and foremost as a face-saving device. The Tiv case, quoted by Gluckman (1965:140), demonstrates some lines of similarity. A woman was taking two goats to the market. On the way she became tired and left the goats in the care of the son of a distant relative. He promised to bring the goats to the market the next day. He did in fact bring one of them, but made some excuses about not having brought the second goat. She brought suit against him. His defense was that she had asked him to bring only one goat to the market and that the other one had died in the meantime. The judges rejected his defense on the grounds that he had not informed the woman that the goat had died. Gluckman's conclusion is that "the court seems to have found an implied contract" (1965:140).

Not only is it not clear what is meant by an "implied contract," since contracts, by definition, are explicit rather than implicit, but in both the Kipsigis and the Tiv cases, the customary standard cited was employed as a means to appeal to the reason of the litigants to accept a given remedy. There can be no contract when the political organization is incapable of enforcing the terms of that contract. There was also no evidence to the effect that these were instances of an agreement of honor. Furthermore, there was no element of a binding arrangement, in which both parties were providing each other with a mutual exchange of goods and services. We are talking here of general standards of obligation rather than specific terms of a contract, which are ultimately enforceable by a court decision. The Tiv share a common characteristic with the Kipsigis in respect to their legal reasoning. Bohannan states, "If Tiv judges make a settlement in which both parties can concur, there is no problem of 'enforcing the decision.' If they do not, they have not, by Tiv definition, 'ended the *jir* satisfactorily.' The correct solution is known to have been found when all the judges and the litigants concur" (1957:65). Bohannan has seemingly reversed the linkage between the variables, and a more plausible statement would read, "Because the Tiv cannot enforce a decision, the judges have to make a settlement to which both parties can concur." Such a decision can only be arrived at on the basis of a concerted appeal to the reasonableness of the litigants, for in the final analysis, it is they who are making the decision.

In the absence of well-defined coercive sanctions, the process of resolving disputes is contingent more on reasoned negotiation than on adjudication. Gulliver has distinguished between these two modes of settlement, but has reduced the element of reasonableness at the expense of stressing the political factor when he says that "the result, the settlement, is in effect some mutually tolerable resolution of the matter in dispute, based on the assessed or demonstrated strengths of the parties" (1969:17). While the relative strengths of the parties may indeed have some influence on the outcome, it is not exclusively a matter of brute force, although force, or potential force, is undoubtedly taken into consideration as a factor in the reasonings of the judges and the litigants. In the long run, however, the argumentation of the judges has to be both reasoned and directed as an appeal toward the reasonableness of the litigants. The Kipsigis, unlike the Arusha Masai studied by Gulliver, cannot call on agnatic kinsmen to support their case in prosecuting or defending a claim, because their patrilineages are dispersed as a consequence of preferred neolocal residence. Thus, the legal process of the Kipsigis is characterized by the balances between the almost equal strengths of individuals within the adversary context of litigation. The following case exemplifies not only this point, but also demonstrates the attempt to arrive at a solution by posing alternative sets of reasonable grounds, which on face value appear to be quite contradictory. Such flexibility would be unheard of in the context of a modern Anglo-American court.

Samuel, an eleven-year-old Baluhiya, ran away from his home and arrived, by chance, at the home of Mosonik Arap Chesimet, who lived in Nandi territory. Arap Chesimet employed Samuel to do odd jobs for a period of one month, after which time he thought it would be a good idea to transfer Samuel to the Kipsigis village of Kiplelji, where Arap Chesimet's father resided. The father, Chesimet Arap Miny, had two wives, the second of whom had no offspring. Samuel was initially informed by Arap Miny that he would be working for him for a salary of 30 shillings per month, which by any reckoning was a ridiculously high salary for an eleven-year-old boy. Samuel accepted this arrangement, and after a few months of work requested his wages. At this point, Arap Miny asked Samuel whether he would be prepared to become his adopted son, which, of course, would release him from the obligation of paying the accumulated wages, as well as provide offspring for the childless second wife, Tabutany. Samuel agreed, and soon after underwent the elaborate Kipsigis initiation procedure. This was bitterly opposed by the two sons of the first wife, Mosonik and Kipkirui Arap Chesimet. They considered that any such formal recognition of Samuel would guarantee his right to an equal share of Arap Miny's estate on the latter's death. All other members of the *kokwet*, however, regarded Samuel as the legal son and heir of Arap Miny, and he assumed the name of Samuel Arap Chesimet on the grounds of his having successfully undergone the initiation ceremony.

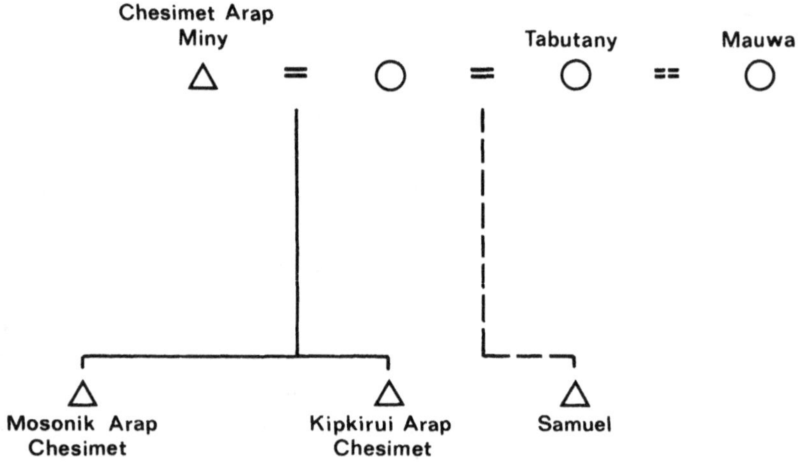

Seven years later there was still some doubt as to the actual status of Samuel vis-à-vis the childless second wife, Tabutany. So Tabutany married another woman, named Mauwa. It is Kipsigis practice that if it is established beyond all doubt that a woman is barren, she has the right to marry another woman. Any children born of the second woman become the children of the first woman, who then assumes the role of a sociological "father" to those children. Tabutany exercised her legitimate right to determine who would have sexual relations with Mauwa, and designated Samuel for that purpose. The only limitation, placed on the choice, is that the man has to be a member of the original husband's subclan (in this case, Arap Miny's subclan). Kipkirui Arap Chesimet objected forcefully. Had he agreed to Samuel having sexual relations with Mauwa, this would have been tantamount to a recognition of Samuel belonging to Arap Miny's subclan. Actually, for the purposes of a claim to inheritance, this would have proven weaker than the claim based on Samuel's status as the adopted son of Tabutany, and it is rather surprising that Kipkirui so violently opposed it, to the extent that he threatened to kill Samuel. Samuel responded in kind and the matter was brought before a widely attended meeting of the judicial forum of the *kokwet*. The *kokwet* is, at one and the same time, both the locally autonomous territorial unit of the Kipsigis and the term applied to the forum of people that deliberates over issues of litigation. Any married man residing in the territorial bounds of the *kokwet* may actively participate in the proceedings of the *kokwet* in its judicial capacity.

Samuel brought the case in order to establish his status as Arap Miny's son. He claimed that his having undergone the initiation ceremony conferred this right on him. This was not an unreasonable point, since everyone had in fact recognized him as such, the ritual having conferred on him Kipsigis "citizenship." Kipkirui argued that at no time had Samuel been formally adopted, but he did not publicly reiterate his threat to kill Samuel in this opening statement. This must have influenced the *kokwet's* decision, which unanimously stated the prevailing public opinion that Samuel was, in fact, Arap Miny's son. Kipkirui publicly rejected this decision and privately informed a number of people that he would make good his threat to kill Samuel. Samuel had no alternative but to counter this by telling people that he would kill Kipkirui first. As it became clear that the prospect of violence between the equally balanced strengths of Kipkirui and Samuel was imminent, the *kokwet* reconvened and came to the following decision: Samuel was *advised* to leave Kiplelji. The choice was up to him, and if he should so decide, he would receive 1,514 shillings in "back pay" from Arap Miny. This was, of course, a total reversal of the principle already established in the *kokwet's* first meeting, but was not perceived as such by the Kipsigis. They saw both solutions as reasonable alternatives.

Samuel immediately agreed to this solution and at first, it appeared that Kipkirui would also go along with it. Now up to this point, Arap Miny had tended to side with his son, Kipkirui, but at the prospect of having to pay out such a large sum of money, he immediately reversed his position and appealed to Samuel to remain as his "son." Samuel, an almost perfect specimen of the reasonable man, was prepared to agree with this on the one condition that Arap Miny would guarantee to restrain Kipkirui from any violence or further threats of violence. Kipkirui then made his one and only concession toward compromise. He was aware of the *kokwet's* hostility toward him, although this had never been openly voiced in *kokwet* sessions. (One can only assume here that Barotse judges would have had a field day in turning moral judgments into standards of reasonableness in this case.) Kipkirui agreed that a portion of the cattle of the second wife, Tabutany, be sold off to raise the 1,514 shillings. This was not too much of a concession on his part, since in any case he would no longer have any vested interest in these cattle once Mauwa gave birth to a male child. Tabutany, on the other hand, refused and sided with Arap Miny by stating that she wanted Samuel to stay on. But the general consensus at the end of the meeting was that Samuel should leave and receive the money.

But a new impasse had now been reached in settling this compromise. Arap Miny did not have the cash to pay Samuel this amount, and a far more complex situation had now arisen as to which cattle would have to be sold in order to raise the money. Kipkirui adamantly opposed any sale of cattle that would result in any potential loss for him on Arap Miny's death. The meeting adjourned in order to allow Arap Miny to find some alternative working arrangement to raise the money. In the interval between this last meeting and the next *kokwet* session, a great deal of argument took place between Arap Miny and his son Kipkirui. The present writer did not observe the exchanges between the two men, nor for that matter was it observed that any other members of the community attempted to interfere in these private exchanges. One of the younger boys in Arap Miny's household reported that Arap Miny had threatened to curse Kipkirui, but that Kipkirui had merely scoffed at the idea. In other cases, it had been noted that these private exchanges in the intervals between *kokwet* sessions often had a decisive bearing on the outcome, although this was not so in this particular case. For when the *kokwet* reconvened two days later, Samuel reiterated his position that he would accept the 1,514 shillings and leave, but the positions of Arap Miny and Kipkirui had not changed in the meantime. The *kokwet* once again formally gave its verdict that Samuel should receive the money and leave, while Arap Miny formally rejected this decision.

At this point, all further attempts to appeal to reasonableness were abandoned, since the Kipsigis now have a convenient egress from an impasse of this nature. Whereas, in the past, the *kokwet* would have reconvened on successive occasions to hammer out a solution, the tendency today is to refer the matter to the magistrate's court when one or both of the parties remain recalcitrant. Since Samuel had no funds to file suit in court, the *kokwet* held an additional session in the presence of the location chief (a civil servant). The purpose of the meeting was to obtain the necessary funds from local government sources so that Samuel could file suit against Arap Miny. The plea was granted and Samuel brought his case to court, but with the proviso of a *kokwet* instruction that Samuel's claim should be over money and not a claim for recognition of status. The magistrate upheld the *kokwet's* decision in his own verdict, and awarded Samuel the full sum of 1,514 shillings. Five months elapsed after this decision and Arap Miny had not yet paid Samuel. Thereupon Samuel obtained an attachment order on Arap Miny's cattle. Kipkirui forestalled this by taking his father's cattle and hiding them somewhere in the Chepalungu forest, or by distributing them among friends within the context of the *kimanagan* cattle lending system. The administrative police were then given the task of recovering these cattle.

In the past, a *kokwet* would transfer a completely irreconcilable dispute to a notable, known as the *kiruogindet neo* or "great judge." This personage had at his command a powerful array of sanctions, mainly supernatural. But insufficient is known as to the extent to which the *kiruogindet neo* reinforced *kokwet* decisions. But the relationship between the *kokwet* and the magistrate's court indicates a subtle, yet clear, influence of the latter on the reasonings of the former. While there is no formal prescription that civil cases have to undergo a prior hearing at the level of the traditional remedy agent before being submitted to the magistrate's court, this is in fact what happens. An analysis of the records of one particular magistrate's court in the Kipsigis area produced the following data: Out of 183 cases tried during a one-year period, 71 percent involved the application of some point of reference to customary law. Thirty-nine out of this group of "customary law" cases were referred back to the *kokwet* for a prior hearing, and out of these thirty-nine cases, ten were actually settled by means of the referral back to the *kokwet*, eighteen were returned back to the court by the *kokwet*, and eleven simply faded away. The magistrate concurred with the decision of the *kokwet* in 59 percent of all the "customary law" cases. In 25 percent of the *kokwet* decisions, the magistrate accepted the decision in principle, but modified the terms of the penalty, and only in 16 percent of these cases did the magistrate overturn the *kokwet*'s decision. There is then an overall awareness among the Kipsigis that the courts tend to provide strong backing for *kokwet* decisions.

One of the consequences of this is that the *kokwet* no longer has to exert itself, with the same diligence as in the past, in searching for compromises acceptable to the canons of reasonableness and the agreement of both parties. There was now the recognition of the probability that most *kokwet* decisions would be backed, and more important, sanctioned, by the court. A clear shift was noted in that there is currently a tendency for the *kokwet* to hand down unilateral decisions in favor of one party and to the exclusion of the other. In three Kipsigis communities studied, one of which had no easy physical access to a court, a clear contrast became apparent. In the remote community, more than 70 percent of the cases that came before the *kokwet* were resolved by means of a form of compromise, whereas in the other two communities in close proximity to a court, only 42 percent and 47 percent of *kokwet*-tried cases were remedied by means of compromise. While judicial rights have not been formally accorded to Kipsigis moots, the element of authority has filtered down from the courts to the *kokwet* in at least a *de facto* sense. As more and more unilateral decisions are handed down as a matter of course through the acquisition of this semiautonomous status, the standards for reasonableness are changing accordingly. Thus, the pragmatism of prior standards of reasonableness, used to achieve compromises, are transposed by more authoritative interpretations of customary law as a new criterion for reasonableness. This supports the contention that shifts toward centralization in the locus of power constitute an important variable in the understanding of reasonableness as a judicial phenomenon. For as authority progressively intervenes, there is decreasingly less reliance on the concept of reasonableness as a mechanism for the resolution of disputes.

In trying to work out the parameters of this mechanical relationship between sovereignty and reasonableness, it appears that when sovereignty is paramount and the judiciary and legislature are one and the same in serving a vested interest in power, there is little recourse to the reasonable man in the form of legal reasoning. An extreme example of this is provided by Rattray in his account of Ashanti[7] law (1929). At the lowest unofficial level of remedy agents, the methods of mediation and conciliation, relying heavily on appeals to reasonableness, would achieve settlements. But the moment a case reached the higher official judicial bodies of the Ashanti, the rules of procedure were governed by extreme formalism and by the threat of equally extreme sanction. Both parties to the dispute were initially considered guilty, even though the matter before the court was what we would understand as a civil issue. Both parties were called on to state their cases and were required to pronounce "the great forbidden name," which in itself is a punishable crime. Witnesses were called to provide testimony under dire oath, and the issue was settled on the chief's assessment of the reliability of the testimony. The man acquitted was the one who won the case, although he was obliged to pay court costs. The loser would later be sentenced, possibly to death, in which event he may also be given the opportunity to ransom himself. Rattray claims that the original procedure in the higher court had grown out of the reconciliation process in the lower court. But,

> it was the growing sense of power, backed by armed authority, which had modified the original procedure. The central authority, once it began to feel its strength, began to welcome litigation and quarrels as a means of raising revenue for the Stool. This was an attitude of the official mind which was the direct antithesis to that found in the original courts. . . . Hence it appears to have come about that the most characteristic feature of these unofficial courts, the *mpata* or conciliation of litigants came to drop out altogether from the higher courts. (1929:386)

This account of the Ashanti from the 1920s serves to place Gluckman's account of the Barotse in a more accurate perspective.

The degree of sovereignty achieved by the Barotse political hierarchy may have been less than that achieved by the Ashanti, but obviously more centralized than the diffuse power structure of the Kipsigis and the Tiv. Gluckman worked predominantly in his ethnographic present, and very little information is provided about the past. What is quite clear is that the colonial authorities had severely limited both the scope of jurisdiction and the former coercive sanctions available for application by the Barotse judiciary. He writes that "the courts have lost the power to inflict certain punishments and remedies, including the death penalty, throttling and unlimited flogging; and they have acquired the power to imprison, an unknown practice in the past" (1955:3). One may deduce from this that prior to the colonial intrusion, the Barotse judiciary formerly operated on a far more authoritarian basis than at the present time. While the colonial influence indirectly accorded more power to the traditional remedy agents of the Kipsigis, it also curtailed the authority of the Barotse courts. Nonetheless, the current sanction of imprisonment and the continued practice of heavy fines set the Barotse apart from the Kipsigis and the Tiv. In Gluckman's Case of the Eloping Wife (1955:113–19), the two defendants are sent to prison until they pay their fines and damages, as decreed by the court. The Barotse cases, given by Gluckman, mostly conclude in a unilateral decision handed down in favor of one of the litigants. There is little attempt to achieve compromises between the disputants, while there is also a clear pattern of authoritarianism in the apportionment of blame and the ensuing liability arising from that blame.

> The *kuta* should not achieve a reconciliation without blaming those who have done wrong. The litigants in coming to court have appealed for a public hearing of the grievances, and these are examined against the norms of behaviour expected of all people. The judges therefore upbraid all the parties where they have departed from their norms. (1955:22)

Different criteria for reasonableness become apparent in the comparison between Kipsigis, Ashanti, and Barotse law. The pragmatism of Kipsigis reasonableness has been linked to the Kipsigis original inability to enforce unilateral decisions. The complete lack of recourse to the concept of reasonableness in the Ashanti process is associated with the high degree of authoritarianism and its possible corollary in corruption. At the higher echelons of the Ashanti judicial process there was no need to find compromises. But the argumentations underlying Barotse legal decisions, the paternalism and moral posturing of the judges may be influenced, in part, by the curtailed authority of these functionaries. Another contributory factor Gluckman has noted is that the "judgements are sermons on filial, parental and brotherly love. This is not inappropriate since the *kuta* is the central administrative chapter for national religious affairs" (1955:22). Lacking case material from the precolonial period, it is virtually impossible to ascertain whether the reasonable man image, extrapolated from Barotse legal decisions, is truly indigenous or might be a mere adaptive response to the 1936 ordinance, which allowed for appeals to British courts. Gluckman notes the "deep resentment" of the Barotse to this decision, and then goes on to point out that "the work of these British courts therefore has to be investigated, as well as the work of new specialized judicial bodies, such as those of the churches" (1955: 27). But by Gluckman's own admission, we learn nothing of this in the rest of the book. MacGaffey's point, reiterated by Chanock, that we cannot isolate traditional customary law from the colonial context within which it operates, is extremely well taken.

The moral stances, assumed by the Barotse judges, could hardly have been impugned by the colonial authorities, and can even be construed as an effective political strategy of the Barotse to maintain their status. There is no evidence to support this assumption. What is clearer, however, is the fact that the high standards of behavior demanded by the Barotse judges invariably allowed them to break down one of the submissions of the case, presented by the litigants, and thus arrive at a unilateral decision. Given this objective, the standards are, if anything, unreasonably high and express ideal rather than reasonable behavior. They are, perhaps, analogous to the *Highway Code* standards of driving. These latter are, in one sense, reasonable propositions, since they undoubtedly serve, at least in theory, to prevent accidents. Most people, however, would regard the perfectionist demand of the *Highway Code* as being unreasonable. In the reality of everyday experience, few, if any, abide by the total complex of rules in the code. On the other hand, the absolute nature of traffic laws does enable the judge to determine guilt with relative ease. This is highly convenient for an overloaded traffic court, which can then handle cases more as a bureaucratic procedure than as a judicial procedure. Thus, the norms underlying both traffic laws and Barotse legal reasoning are, perhaps, intrinsically reasonable statements as to how people ought to behave. Yet their inflexible application, with so little leeway at the level of the judicial process, appear, paradoxically, to be quite unreasonable.

That which now has the force of law in determining the reasonable behavior of Barotse in their different statuses encompasses presumably acceptable norms from the past. The relationship between norms and law has been discussed by Bohannan.

> All institutions (including legal institutions) develop customs. Some customs, in some societies, are re-institutionalized at another level; they are restated for the more precise purposes of legal institutions. When this happens, therefore, law may be regarded as a custom that has been restated in order to make it amenable to the activities of the legal institutions. (1965:35–36)

The operative concepts in Bohannan's argument are in the phrases "restated for the precise purposes of legal institutions" and "to make it more amenable to the activities of the legal institutions." It is not implied here that the outcome of the restatement is any the less reasonable; it is merely an alternative authoritarian predetermination of what constitutes reasonableness. Its terms are more precisely defined for the purposes of legal institutions in comparison with its relatively undefined format of a felt norm or a shared understanding. An example of this may be seen in Cotran's work on the law panels of Kenya (1963). In many tribes, the abuse of a member of a higher age grade was, in the past, a serious offense. It was a generalized proposition, constituting a shared understanding that was meaningful in the context of a noncentralized polity. The law panels transformed this original rationalization, which was concerned with matters of respect and disrespect, into a different concept. It is qualitatively different, even though it is no less reasonable in its new context. Abuse is now held to be an offense, not because it is a form of disrespect but because it is likely to cause physical violence, or in more formal terms, a breach of the peace. If disrespect is no longer the criterion determining reasonableness, then it made sense to extend the provision beyond the abuse directed by a junior toward a senior, to include all abuse whatsoever. One suggested version of the restated custom reads, "Any person who intentionally insults or abuses and thereby gives provocation to any person, intending it, or knowing it to be likely that, such provocation will cause a breach of the peace, is guilty of an offence."

But the transformation is more than the mere change in substantive content. For while the shared understanding of a norm is, in one sense, an appeal to the reasonableness of the individual to behave in a certain kind of way, its reformulation into a law provides another dimension in which appeals to reasonableness play no significant role. It is a dimension, in which validity is sought not at the level of meaningful social categories, but rather in terms of *a priori* assumptions that constitute the basis of a logical system. As Ross wrote in the preface to his work, *Towards a Realistic Jurisprudence*, "the law belongs at the same time to the world of empirical facts and the supersensual world of the eternal ideas, the realm of validity" (1946:9–10).

Notes

1. Llewellyn and Hoebel are the co-authors of the classical legal-anthropological study *The Cheyenne Way*. Law students have traditionally been obliged to read this book as they have similarly been obliged to read Malinowski's *Crime and Custom in Savage Society*. Llewellyn, as the senior author, brought his jurisprudential knowledge to bear on the fieldwork data supplied by Hoebel. Even if the book tends to idealize the legal "genius" of the Cheyenne, its contribution, nonetheless, is the application of the case method to the study of law—in this instance, the study of primitive law. The material influenced Llewellyn's subsequent development of his "law-jobs" theory as one of the basic postulates of American legal realism. Llewellyn was particularly impressed by what he considered to be their remarkable capacity for creative problem solving. The Cheyenne are a tribe within the wider grouping of the Plains Indians. They effectively adapted to the introduction of the horse into their material culture, and engaged in buffalo hunting as a major economic activity. Population density shifted on a seasonal basis, from dispersed bands in the autumn and winter to a dense convocation of all the Cheyenne bands in the late

spring for the purpose of ritual activity. Organized in basic units of bands, the Cheyenne had a bilateral kinship structure that, by definition, laid no emphasis on unilineal descent groups. The bands had political representation in the Council of Forty-Four, which made major political decisions. But the lodges of the military associations were the prime agents for the resolution of internal disputes on an everyday basis, and their decisions carried significant weight with the Council of Forty-Four. The Cheyenne engaged in elaborate rituals, foremost among which were the Sun Dance and the Sacred Arrow Renewal Ceremony, the dominant theme being the renewal of resources.

2. The Barotse *kuta*, most appropriately translated as "council," performs both political and judicial functions. In the present study it is referred to solely in its judicial capacity. The paramount ruler does not usually sit in its sessions, and the *kuta* consists of three sets of differentially ranked councillors: (a) headmen or nonroyal chiefs, (b) royal officers or stewards, and (c) princes and prince-consorts. Each one of these groups is ranked within itself. Opinions are given in sequence from the most junior to the most senior in the ranking system. Litigants present their cases and are subject to examination by the members of the *kuta*. The Lozi have developed an extensive terminology for classifying evidence as interested or disinterested evidence, direct or circumstantial evidence, and hearsay. They look for corroboration and employ various tests for weighing evidence. Relying heavily on the evidence, the *kuta* bases its reasonings on measuring the evidence against standards of reasonableness in order to arrive at what they consider to be an impartial solution.
3. Malinowski's *Crime and Custom in Savage Society* is based on fieldwork conducted by Malinowski in the Trobriand Islands of Melanesia. The Trobrianders are horticulturalists and fishermen. Trading relationships are institutionalized in the *kula* ring, a classical model of reciprocity as a motivating force in economic activity. The Trobrianders are organized within four major matriclans that comprise several landowning subclans. A paramount chief marries into several subclans, by so doing cementing ramified relationships throughout the society and also extending his political influence. Like other lower-level chiefs in the society, he maintains his position by judiciously redistributing the wealth received in tribute. While the chief's status is high and many privileges accrue to that status, he had little in the way of coercive sanctions at his disposal to back up his political decisions. His perceived control over the supernatural allows for the use of supernatural sanctions, including the withholding of his ritual powers. This is occasionally made more explicit by his employment of sorcerers against offenders. His position lies somewhere between that of a formal state ruler and what has been described by Sahlins as the "Big Man." The lack of formal authoritarian attributes has its effects on Trobriand legal thinking.

4. No claim is being made that Busoga society is feudal in the sense of the characteristic feudalism of England. The common factors obtaining in both situations are first, a political, dominant-subordinate relationship based on the personal allegiance of a man to his ruler and second, a reciprocal relationship based on the provision of service in exchange for the use of land.
5. The Kipsigis maintain a mixed economy based on traditional cattle herding, the growing of maize and potatoes, and in recent years, the cash crop cultivation of tea. The Kipsigis are organized in dispersed patrilineages, dispersed mainly as a consequence of the practice of neolocal residence on marriage. They live in virtually autonomous territorial units known as *kokwet*. The term *kokwet* applies not only to the territorial unit itself, but also to any economic cooperative unit that emerges on an *ad hoc* basis within the local community. Its third application is to the local judicial forum that resolves disputes. The Kipsigis form an acephalous society, in which there are no well-defined political functionaries. An age-set system performs political functions insofar as members of the senior sets exercise considerable influence in any decision-making process. The establishment of a national system of courts has strengthened the *kokwet*'s ability to render judicial decisions based on indigenous customary law by supplying sanctions that, in the past, were lacking.
6. The Tiv are a society living in central Nigeria. Bohannan has described their economy, which is a subsistence sphere that produces yams, cereals, and vegetables, in addition to which small livestock are maintained. Above the subsistence level surpluses are marketed. There is also a prestige sphere of economic activity, the commodities of which are cattle, slaves, cloth, medicines, ritual offices, and metal rods. The last constitutes a form of "currency." All items within the prestige sphere are exchangeable and can be used for brideprice. Only under very dire circumstances are they employed in exchange for subsistence items. Today, monetary exchange has considerably modified the traditional economic patterns, as is true for everywhere. The Tiv political organization is based on segmentary lineages. The local territorial units are patrilineages that stand in segmental opposition to one another. Since theoretically all Tiv are descended from a common ancestor, the segmented lineages are components of wider descent groupings. Disputing segments are usually of equal strengths, which means that ideally the resolution of the dispute can be achieved through negotiations in which other noninvolved segments can act as peacekeepers. The Tiv have moots, known as *jir*. These moots do not function in an adjudicative capacity, and the resolution of disputes before the moot is hammered out by the participating elders through negotiation and compromise. The threat of supernatural sanctions is one mechanism employed in order to influence the litigants.

7. In addition to agricultural production, the Ashanti engaged in very extensive external trade, mainly as a consequence of the availability of kola and gold in their territory. Ashanti are organized in matrilineages, the elected heads of which, themselves, elect a divisional chief. Over time the Ashanti became a highly politically centralized society. The process of centralization began at the end of the seventeenth century and maintained its independence until the defeat of the Ashanti by the British at the end of the nineteenth century. Despite centralization, local units always had a degree of autonomy in dealing with local affairs. The social order was reinforced by the belief in the lineage ancestors' ability to promote the group's welfare. Each lineage has a symbolic stool, which is in effect a shrine for the local ancestors. By the same token, the ancestors of the royal lineage guard the interests and well-being of the kingdom as a whole. Thus a ruler, as guardian of the stool, combines both secular and religious functions. The British conquest of the territory led to the creation of the Kingdom of the Ashanti, ruled by the former chief of the Kumasi district. The Kingdom was symbolized by the Golden Stool, which demanded the allegiance of all Ashanti.

3

Scandinavian and American Legal Realism: Measures of Reasonableness?

The concluding sentence of the last chapter (the quotation from Ross) appropriately establishes the terms of reference for this chapter by virtue of its contradictory implications. The Uppsala philosophers[1] totally rejected what they considered to be a metaphysical basis of the law. By this they meant that, for example, when the law speaks of *rights*, these same rights have no verifiable objective existence. If rights are merely the subjective product of a man's thought, then they truely belong to the realm of the metaphysical. But the contradiction lies in the fact that the metaphysical still has an important role to play in the real world, for the political powers-that-be in any society manipulate the metaphysical in order to exact conformity to a set of rules. When a judge states that "this is valid and that is void," that "this is reasonable and that is unreasonable," most people believe that this is *in fact* the case. Language is the tool of the lawyer. It can transcend reality by describing the unreal. Legal language becomes a manipulative tool in the hands of its practitioners, for among other things it evokes emotive responses. People are convinced by combinations of words. This is the suggested avenue for the objective empirical analysis advocated by the realists. It can take one of two possible directions: How does the human brain operate in response to the stimulus of words? How are the motives and beliefs of persons manipulated by others, whatever the purpose? The answer to the first question is as yet unknown. Lévi-Strauss has rightly surmised that only progress in neurophysiology and biochemistry will enable us to understand how the brain actually operates. But the second question can be dealt with empirically. It concerns the conceptual representation of processes in social reality, even though the underlying mechanical causes remain unknown.

If these propositions have any merit, they should be subjected to cross-cultural examination, which is precisely what the legal realists did *not* do. Both the Scandinavian and American schools of legal realism have raised questions that ought to concern anthropologists of law. But among the realists, apart from Llewellyn, who together with Hoebel had done anthropological fieldwork among the Cheyenne Indians, members of either movement have paid little more than lip service to empirical anthropological findings. The Scandinavian realists' ascription of legal validity to magical beliefs in primitive society is unsatisfactory. We have already noted that the recognition of mutuality is a powerful a motivating force as is magic, if not more so. Furthermore, they have circumscribed the relevance of actual behavior to mean the behavior of contemporary courts. For example, one of the discussions of the Scandinavian legal realists rests on whether the element of coercion employed by the courts is the dominant factor in determining legal validity. Any behavior occurring outside of the legal institutions is considered irrelevant. Aubert, commenting on Ross, writes,

> The decisive factor determining that the prohibition is valid law is solely the fact that it is effectively upheld by the courts where breaches of law are brought to light and prosecuted. It makes no difference whether people comply with or frequently ignore the prohibition. This indifference results in the apparent paradox that the more effectively a rule is complied with in extrajudicial life, the more difficult it is to ascertain whether the rule possesses validity, because the courts have that much less opportunity to manifest their reaction. (1983:12)

This point has already been alluded to above in the discussion of the role of reasonableness in the standards of the highway code, as reflected in the traffic laws, and its consistent nonobservance in everyday life. Wherein lies the validity of the highway code? Is it merely a measure by means of which one judge finds a driver to have acted unreasonably and another judge claims that the standards of perfection required by the Code are unreasonable under certain circumstances? The fact that people are constantly disregarding the code in their everyday behavior is a sociological fact of absolutely no consequence whatsoever for the court. It also makes little difference if the judge believes that by punishing traffic offenders he is successfully reducing traffic accidents. Compliance or noncompliance with the law has nothing to do with its validity.

The arguments of the legal realists lend support to the overall contention of this work, that if the reasonable man ever existed in some pristine state, in a Malinowskian sense, he has been supplanted by the reasonable or unreasonable judge, who works within the constraints of the system, of which he is also a part. While Hart left the connection between primary rules of obligation and secondary rules of recognition[2] as something implicit, the realists have tried to make this connection more explicit by turning to the role of the judge. And so, Ross writes,

> A national law system, considered as a valid system of norms, can accordingly be defined as the norms which actually are operative in the mind of the judge, because they are felt by him to be socially binding and therefore obeyed. The test of the validity is that on this hypothesis—that is accepting the norms as a scheme of interpretation—we can comprehend the actions of the judge (the decisions of the court) as meaningful responses to given conditions. (1958:35)

There are a number of elements implicit in the thinking of the Scandinavian legal realists that ought to be made more explicit. The element of coercion, while undeniably playing an important role, is also insufficient in explaining the behavior of the judge in the handing down of his decisions. If Ross's contention is correct, that "we can comprehend the actions of the judge as meaningful responses to given conditions," then we have to admit the existence of another relevant element, which is the complex of ideas, beliefs, and feelings as experienced by people.

The founding father of the philosophical position adopted by the Scandinavian legal realists was Hagerstrom. His overall contention was that people *believed* that they had rights and duties, even though these rights and duties have no objective standing in reality (1953). It is the belief itself that concerns us, as a factor that conditions behavior. The element of coercion merely reinforces that belief. If I claim that I have a *right* to security, it is in fact a meaningless claim. I could, perhaps, back it up in metaphysical terms by saying that it is a God-given right, but that, of course, does not accord it any more objective reality. Even when the legal system supports my right by restraining those who infringe upon it, it is doing nothing more than bolstering my belief in the existence of the right rather than objectifying it. Judges share the same outlook as everyone else by believing in the existence of rights and duties, and they promote that belief by virtue of their decisions. Rights and duties are important points of reference in mapping out the topography of reasonableness, but by the same token, reasonableness is also an article of faith that has no objective standing. The same holds true for norms. The statement of a norm is merely an expression of a belief, of a feeling, that people ought to behave in certain kinds of ways. There is a considerable discrepancy between the statements in regard to how people *ought* to behave and how they actually *do* behave.

The Scandinavian legal realists sometimes confuse the issues in the formulation of their questions, even if the general drift of the questions appears to be correct. For example, Olivecrona, when explaining the issue of a law's validity, is really asking why people obey laws. This point is made by MacCormack, who in answering this question in terms used by the Scandinavian school, states, "Basically there are two reasons for obedience to those independent imperatives which are rules of law. The first is the existence of coercive machinery within the state and the second is the psychological reaction of the members of the society" (1970:40). The element of coercion obviously has little or nothing to do with reasonableness. On the other hand, the psychological reactions of the members of society toward laws merit some evaluation as to their relative reasonableness. If people obey laws solely to prevent the unpleasant consequences of the sanctions imposed because of their infringement, then there is no need to search for validity beyond Austin's dogma of the "will of the sovereign." But if compliance with the law is also a function of people's substantive assessment of a law, then we have to consider whether that assessment is made on the basis of the criterion of the reasonableness of a given law. Those persons who, for example, are diligently obeying the *Highway Code*, may be doing so for a variety of reasons—altruism or a rational sense of self-preservation, both of which involve considerations of reasonableness. On the other hand, there are those who are complying solely out of fear of being subjected to punitive sanctions. Those who do not comply presumably consider that the standards of perfection demanded of them are unreasonable, the other alternative being that the chances of being caught are slight. The behavior of drivers is extremely complex, since it takes into account all of the aforementioned factors in making instant decisions to immediate circumstances. Traffic offenses are also different from other offenses, since in most cases they lack the element of predetermination, given the rapidity of changing circumstances.

One of the basic tenets of legal realism is that the validity of a law is to be seen in the actions of the court. Validity is accorded to the rule by the decisions of the court, and there is no doubt that the element of coercion serves to reinforce that validity. It makes the valid appear concrete. But the critics of legal realism legitimately ask whether a law in the statute books, which has never been applied in court, is any less valid in its standing as a law. The answer to this question can be seen in one or the other of two logical alternatives. Either the law is being universally obeyed and its validity, therefore, never has to be tested in the framework of a court, or the authorities, for any number of reasons, are reluctant to bring cases of infringement of the law to the courts. A third possibility is that people are, in fact, breaking the law and are not being apprehended, but this will not be considered here. In either instance we can fall back on an explanation in terms of reasonableness. If everybody were to obey the law, to the extent that no case is ever brought to court, we may suggest that the reason for the universal obedience is that people are accepting, or at least are not questioning, the reasonableness of that law. Alternatively, if the authorities countenance the infringement of a law by not bringing the case to court, this may be because the law is being deemed unreasonable, under the given circumstances, by the authorities themselves.

Returning to the overall argument of the Scandinavian realists that legal validity has no objective standing, we still remain with the fact that people believe in the objective validity of laws. In the absence of any body of empirical knowledge that would serve to prove or falsify a legal rule, only belief objectifies its validity. A legal rule, unlike a physical law, is not subject to empirical proof. It is the belief itself that becomes the object of sociological analysis. Whereas in the past a metaphysical basis was explicitly ascribed to validity (the *divine right* of rulers to promulgate laws, for example) the acceptance of validity today finds its grounding in terms of *reason, rationality*, or occasionally, *morality and justice*, all of these being relative and no more objective than *divinity*. So again, we are in fact dealing with people's beliefs about law rather than the law itself.

Obviously a law is not a mere linguistic construction, in the form of a directive, completely detached from any kind of social reality. Ross correctly states that it is "a directive which corresponds in a particular way to certain social facts" (1958:82). If indeed there is a normative element underlying certain types of rules, it follows that in the vast majority of instances people are conforming to the norm. The mistake sociologists make in inferring the existence of norms, is the assumption of sufficiency in their method of establishing the existence of norms through the observation of recurrent patterns of behavior. Ross seizes upon the absence of the additional component of the normative aspect of the rule by pointing out, "For it is necessary for the establishment of a norm that it be followed not only with external regularity, that is with observable conformity with the rule, but also with the consciousness of following a rule and being bound to do so" (1968: 83).

It is here that we return once again to the unresolved question of whether rules are obeyed out of fear of coercive sanctions (in the event of their infringement), or whether there is a positive feeling of compulsion to obey rules, which Ross terms "the experience of validity." But leaving aside the question of validity and addressing only the issue of whether people feel a compulsion to obey rules, MacCormack makes an important differentiation between "the feeling that one is bound by a rule and a statement that a rule is binding" (1970:47). MacCormack cites two of the Scandinavian legal realists on this issue. Olivecrona asserts that to say that a rule is binding refers to the belief that the behavior prescribed by the rule possesses a nonexistent quality—that of being binding. Ross is more specific in stating that the rule possesses some moral quality in that it conforms with what is required by God or by reason.

The overall error in the Scandinavian realists' analysis is the attempt to establish a relationship between validity, on the one hand, and feelings and other psychological phenomena, on the other. If the question is circumscribed as to why people obey or disobey laws, then the remaining portions of the realists' arguments begin to make sense. If the question is phrased in this manner, one may assume (on hypothetical grounds) that at least one of the relevant factors is that people obey laws because they consider them to be reasonable. By the same token, there are clear instances of people breaking laws when they consider them to be unreasonable, such as rebellion, conscientious objection, civil disobedience, and highly inconvenient standards of perfection. In these cases the perpetrators are expressing their skepticism about the reasonableness of existing laws, and, by the same token, they are basing their actions on some perceived alternative criteria of reasonableness.

It follows then, that courts, in upholding the laws, are no less motivated by the psychological compulsion to obey laws than is the average and reasonable citizen. When a judge hands down a decision, he is in fact making an evaluative social comment on people's behavior. One cannot evaluate the *validity* of a law—it is either valid or invalid. What the court is ultimately doing is evaluating *behavior* by the standards set by laws in terms of what is right or wrong, what ought or ought not to be done, and what is to be considered reasonable. One of the by- products of this is the correctness of the legal realists' statement that the validity of a law is established by the recurrent behavior of the courts, thus making validity a social fact rather than an abstract legal proposition. Thus there appears to be a link between the concepts of validity and reasonableness.

A judge's assessment of the reasonableness of behavior, in the light of norms, is an integral part of the judicial process. People go to court in order to receive satisfaction in the pursuit of furthering what they believe to be their rights. Like validity, rights have no objective standing in the real world. People *believe* they have rights. But if we assume a functional approach to the concept of rights, then at least one of its functions is that rights confer powers. Consequently, if the court, in determining rights, is in fact conferring powers, the test of reasonableness is actually applied to that functional objectification of the feelings underlying rights. The Scandinavians were forced into a situation of choosing between the association of rights with primitive magical beliefs (Hagerstrom, 1953) or claiming that rights constituted the "objectification of feelings" (Olivecrona, 1959:143). Ross attempts to exist from this impasse by the ill-founded techniques of the nineteenth-century evolutionists by speculating that primitive man rationalized his epistemological understanding of rights as having a basis in magical powers. On the other hand, modern man falsely believes that he has rights, in an objective sense, because these rights are given linguistic expression in rules and laws that, in turn, accord powers to men. Ross stresses the mystical power of the *word* as a part of human behavior. In the same vein, Weber has pointed out that the ideal-type category of the formal rational lays emphasis on the fulfillment of certain symbolic acts, like saying "I do" in the marriage ceremony, or the formal acts involved in the writing of a will. There are undoubtedly anachronistic elements in modern law that might indicate, in a speculative sense, an element of continuity from the formal irrational (e.g., oath taking) to the formal rational. In either case, the validity accorded to the legal act is a function of deep-seated beliefs. The overall conclusion appears to remain that the law rests ultimately on a set of beliefs to the effect that both people and judges believe the law to be valid per se. The argument offered here challenges the assumptions of the mystical power of the *word* and the magical basis of the *belief*, and offers an alternative proposition that people's beliefs in the validity of a law is conditioned by their perception of whether the law accords to any reasonable standard of behavior or not. This idea may, perhaps, be too optimistic in that it ascribes the attribute of common sense to human beings.

Beyond the rejection of the idea of a self-contained logical legal system, there appears to be little in common between the Scandinavian and American schools of legal realism. While the orientation of the Scandinavians was more in the nature of an eclectic inquiry into the philosophy of law, the American realists were concerned with the more technical aspects of the existing law. Legal terminology, such as rights, rules, and validity, are seen by the Scandinavians as words that trigger a cognitive response in the listeners or readers. The Americans, on the other hand, limited themselves to regarding the same terminology as descriptors of judicial behavior. But this difference only serves to highlight the basic problem of where lies the locus of the concept of reasonableness in legal discourse. Is reasonableness implicit in people's beliefs concerning the validity of law? Or, as shall also be demonstrated, is reasonableness to be found in the actions of judges, which, if so, brings us back to the original contention that there are no reasonable men, only reasonable or unreasonable judges.

The American movement of legal realism is selectively reviewed here in terms of two of its major protagonists: Frank's psychological perspective, and Llewellyn's standpoint on the practical skills of judging. Like any school of thought, American realism neither came into being *ex nihilo* nor existed in a vacuum. It was a strong reaction against the traditional conservatism of the American judiciary. It picked up on, and went further than, Pound's sociological jurisprudence, which was in itself a critique of that same conservatism. Yet at the same time, it was different from Pound's approach, since it lacked any systematic attempt to construct a theoretical basis. In essence, Llewellyn was advocating a "commonsense" approach to the skill of judging, an advocacy bordering on the nontheoretical but closely associated with the concept of reasonableness. Hunt has pointed out that while both Llewellyn's and Frank's common point of departure was agreement over the basic lack of certainty in law, Frank's relativism was based on the indeterminacy of establishing facts, whereas the skepticism of Llewellyn and others was directed toward the rules themselves (1978:43). Frank was extreme in his antitheoretical perspective against legal science, while Llewellyn conceded that law was nonetheless an orderly discipline in its own right, at least from the point of view of its more technical aspects. If Llewellyn leaned toward any kind of theory at all, it was toward the trend that was developing in American sociology at that time—structural functionalism. Without realizing the logical and substantive imperfections of that particular sociological theory, Llewellyn could easily move on to the analysis of the functions of the court and to coin the term "law jobs," which for him became the essence of the law itself. From here, Llewellyn made a series of intellectual jumps, without regard to standards of logical rigor, and coined additional concepts such as "law ways," "law stuff," and "law craft." Llewellyn's ideas on "law craft" are of specific relevance to the idea of reasonableness. Hunt writes,

> This concern with "craftsmanship" in law provides a major mediating theme in Llewellyn's work. His exuberance and enchantment with the "success" of the Cheyenne in resolving trouble cases is thereby linked with his espousal of the "Grand Style" as the appropriate craft technique for appellate judging under contemporary social conditions, for which he argues mightily in *The Common Law Tradition*. (1978:50)

When Llewellyn addressed himself to the idea of *style*, he was referring specifically to the modes of thought employed by judges and certainly not to the linguistic or literary aspects of their work. In keeping with the overall ideological position of the realist movement, "Grand Style" was advocated in distinction to its opposite mode of thought—"Formal Style." Twining has summed up in an efficient table the basic differences between Grand and Formal styles as modes of legal thought (1973:212). All the defining characteristics of the Grand Style allow for the employment of canons of reasonableness into the argumentation of the judges, while the Formal style nullifies this possibility. This may be exemplified by some of the characteristics cited by Twining. If, in terms of the Formal style, the model of the legal rule takes the form of "If x, then y," it follows that the judge needs no recourse to reasonableness in order to argue his decision. But in the framework of the Grand style, Llewellyn allows for the overall argument of "If x, then y," but adds on the qualification that this formula has to overtly fulfill the functions of "producing effects z" or "remedying mischief z" and, thus, cites z as the reason underlying the decision. The necessity to substantively clarify z would require the judge to consider the reasonableness of x, among other things. The underlying principle distinguishing the Formal from the Grand style is that in the former a general rule is being employed as a premise for a syllogism, whereas in the latter, Llewellyn is advocating a general proposition embodying a policy, the function of which is to guide rather than to control interpretation.

Again, if one is talking about guidance rather than control, and a proposition rather than a rule, then the factor of reasonableness has an important role to play. The American legal realists emphasized fact skepticism rather than rule skepticism, for in the latter instance, while the rule itself may be absolutely clear, doubts may arise as to its correct application in any given situation. On the other hand, the grand style has to pay more attention to the dubiousness inherent in the facts of the case, which, in turn, implies greater reliance on standards of reasonableness as a means to assess the facts. In Twining's summation of the realist position, a court employing the Formal style would "discover and declare the applicable rule and apply it to the facts of the case" (1973:213). In comparison, a Grand style court would "resolve the doubt according to wisdom, justice and situation sense within the leeways accorded by the authoritative sources," as well as "providing guidance for the future" (ibid., 213).

The significant terms here are *wisdom, justice, situation sense, reason*, and *leeways*. Twining rightly points out the difficulty in trying to understand these concepts and the inconsistencies incurred in any attempt to account for them. Llewellyn engages in semantic gymnastics in an attempt to explain himself. Twining demonstrates this by quoting from Llewellyn, "*Only as a judge or court knows* the facts of life, *only as they truely understand* those facts of life, *only as they have it in them to rightly evaluate those facts and to fashion rightly a sound rule* and an apt remedy . . . " (1960:217). This is Llewellyn's version of the meaning of "situation sense," and Twining critically assesses this by asking, "How does one recognize 'true understanding' of the facts and 'right evaluation' of them? What are the criteria for determining 'right evaluation', 'right fashioning', a 'sound rule'"? (1973:217).

The answer is that one cannot construct criteria for these purposes. One can only feel some sympathy toward Llewellyn and, perhaps, begin to understand the impact that the experience among the Cheyenne had upon him. The Cheyenne had successfully implemented their felt norms into an intuitive assessment of the facts of the case. This would not make a particularly convincing argument for the professional lawyers, to whom Llewellyn was addressing his written works. Llewellyn would have made a far more powerful case, had he used the concept of reasonableness instead of the specific terms that he chose to use. No lawyer could deny that the use of the word *reasonable* is a recurring feature of many modern judicial decisions. Contemporary judges use the word *reasonable* and few question the right of the judge to use the term in arriving at his decision, for it is in the framework of the judge's judicial discretion that the grand or formal styles of judging are adopted. While certain facets of reasonableness have been defined in precedent, other facets rely solely on the judge's intuitive ability to evaluate behavior.

It is the American realists' emphasis on the facts of the case, rather than on the search for the relevant rule, that brings the concepts of *situation sense* and *reasonableness* into close proximity. The realists of both Scandinavian and American persuasions were correct in assuming that the law is what the courts do. The nonscientific element of the judge's work is his evaluation of the facts of the case, the recourse to argument by analogy, and the attempt to fit the facts into established categories. Judges appear to be prone to use the term *reasonable*, when the linkage between the facts of the case and the appropriate law is not patently clear. Some judges use the term automatically, without any additional clarification. Other judges explain what they mean when they use the term. Courts, therefore, are contending with the issue of reasonableness, but with an occasional differential emphasis on its meaning as a pure and simple function of the individual judge's personal world view. The contribution of the realists is surely to be seen in their debunking of the myth of a legal science.

The idea of reasonableness is always implicit in Llewellyn's exhortations to the judiciary. In a recipelike approach to the craft of judging, Llewellyn advocates that the judge should initially assess facts as a layman would, to try to see the normal working of things and discover how it broke down in the light of the specific dispute. At the next stage, it is incumbent on the judge to categorize the facts of the case into *socially meaningful categories*, which, of course, stands in stark contrast to predetermined legal categories. At this point Llewellyn brings into play the concept of situation sense. Situation sense requires the positing of categories that have a narrower scope than the broader categories used by the law. Every situation provides its own special set of significant circumstances, and something is inevitably lost in their overall inclusion within a broader category. If we talk in terms of the category "employer-employee" relationship, the comparative situations of a factory worker vis-à-vis the factory owner is significantly different from that of a university professor vis-à-vis the university's administration. While there may be common grounds for reasonable expectations in both instances, the nature of disputes in either case may require the application of differential criteria of reasonableness for assessing the facts of the dispute.

Llewellyn advocated openness as the hallmark of articulated judicial reasoning. The judge should declare his value judgments, since it is inevitable that latent value judgments creep into judicial decision making. This has been demonstrated most clearly by J. A. G. Griffith in his book *The Politics of the Judiciary*. When a judge cites reasonableness as an integral part of the logic of his justification for a given decision, he is invoking not only his own motivations but is also assessing the motivations of others. The logic involved in the justification of a decision is not, and cannot be, the logic of logicians, since factors extraneous to the parameters of induction, deduction, and even recourse to argument by analogy are relevant to the judicial process. If what Llewellyn is arguing is true, the judicial process is not dealing solely with points of law but is actually dealing with a myriad of facts in infinite sets of situational combinations. The relative weakness and strength of the legal system lies in the varying skill of judges in the ways they categorize these facts as an integral part of the logic of justification. The fundamental difference between a scientific assessment of facts and a judicial assessment of those same facts lies in that lawyers argue by analogy and, as a consequence, move inconsistently between different levels of abstraction. Facts in one case may be reassigned to different abstracted categories in other cases. This can sometimes occur even in the judge's summing up within the same case. A court, unlike a laboratory, is an open system, in which the measure of control over the facts, as well as their combination with other facts, is minimal. In the framework of the formula "If *x*, then *y*," skepticism has to be directed toward *x*—not just the facts themselves, but also their categorization—since *y* is already given as a constant legal proposition. Although every judge determines the nature of the relevant facts within the leeways of his judicial discretion, he also often has to make a value judgment as to whether the behavior underlying the facts was reasonable or not. At this point the question arises whether the judge is still acting as a lawyer, or whether he is perhaps playing the role of a layman psychologist.

As already indicated, Llewellyn was more of a rule skeptic than Frank, who assumed the role of the fact skeptic. Both of them were undoubtedly fact skeptics, but the difference in their emphases emerged from their respective interests in different types of courts. Llewellyn was concerned with the activities of appeals courts, in which matters of "rule" were the prime issue, while Frank directed his attention toward the trial courts, where matters of "fact" ultimately constituted the outcome. Frank's ideas, prolifically stated in the many items of his published work, are all brought together in one volume entitled *Courts on Trial*. As the ultimate fact skeptic, Frank argues for the uniqueness of each case in terms of its factual content. Furthermore, the idiosyncracies of all parties to the case—the litigants, witnesses, lawyers, judges, and juries—will yield *perceptions* of the facts, rather than the facts themselves. Irrespective of the rules, these perceptions of the facts will logically render the outcome unpredictable. Frank's impeachment goes even further when he cites the adversary procedure as an almost inevitable precondition for the distortion of the facts. According to Frank, the adversary procedure militates against the court's attempt to arrive at the truth. Witnesses are primed by counsel, are favorably predisposed toward the party that requires their testimony, and are sometimes even declared "hostile" in the absence of this predisposition. The cogency of Frank's argument lies in the issue that the judge really has no objective technique for establishing the truth of the facts. Frank's own solutions to this problem are either impractical—the use of psychologists in the analysis of testimony or the changing of the curriculum of legal education to include the social sciences—or gratuitous, since the subjective perceptions of facts can never reveal the truth to any high degree of exactitude.

This being the case, the trial judge can do little more than make his own subjective appraisal of the already subjective perception of the facts that have been brought before him. After ruling out contradictions, inconsistencies, and impossibilities, the judge is still left with a body of "facts," which he is obliged to evaluate. Furthermore, Frank suggests that the logic of judicial reasoning is, apparently, first to arrive at a decision, and then to work backward by citing the appropriate fact provided by the testimony, to which the appropriate rule is then applied (1949:168). The weak link in the whole process, therefore, is the trial judge's determination of what is, or what is not, fact. The range of choices before him in making this determination is somewhat limited. He can either believe or not believe the evidence that has been presented to him. Where the issues are clear and the evidence is incontrovertible, the decision making is not particularly problematic. When two sets of conflicting testimony of equal consistency are submitted to the judge, he can only evaluate them in terms of their relative plausibility. It is at this point that he will be obliged to employ, at least as part of the evaluative process, the test of reasonableness. Does one version of the evidence appear to be more reasonable than the other? While the judge may, as Frank suggests, evaluate the factual evidence by looking at such "fireside equities" as the demeanor, personality, and character of the witness as factors that could possibly serve to bolster credibility, it is ultimately the innate reasonableness or unreasonableness of the judge that governs the selection or rejection of facts.

It is not surprising, therefore, given the arguments of both the fact skeptics and the rule skeptics, that judges fall back on the ubiquitous use of the concept of reasonableness. The frequency of the use of the term *reasonableness* increases in direct proportion to the "hardness" of the case. Its use has been described here as ubiquitous, not only for its frequency, but also because its nonspecificity conceals a plethora of motivations such as policies, principles, personal idiosyncracies, ideologies, and standards of morality. In modern systems of law, the concept of reasonableness sometimes takes the form of a designed obfuscation, either when it appears as a component in the actual statement of the law, or as a component in the judge's verdict. In the former instance, a case in point is *Liversidge v. Anderson* (1941).[3]

The secretary of state was empowered by the Defence Regulations of 1939 to detain someone, when he had "*reasonable cause to believe* a person to be of hostile associations" (italics mine). The appellant claimed that "the court must confine itself to the construction of the regulation and the secretary of state must satisfy the court that he had reasonable cause to believe. . . . " The court dismissed the plea on the grounds that it had no jurisdiction over the secretary of state's executive decision. Of the five judges deliberating on this case, two may be singled out for comparison in their attitudes toward reasonableness. Lord Macmillan states,

> To require that a cause of belief shall be reasonable necessarily implies a reference to some standard of reasonableness. Is the standard of reasonableness which must be satisfied an impersonal standard independent of the Secretary of State's own mind, or is it the personal standard of what the Secretary of State himself deems reasonable?

Macmillan, in answering his own question, engages in casuistry,

> Had the phrase run in impersonal form—"If there is reasonable cause to believe"—there would have been more justification for maintaining there was no ambiguity, though I should not even so regard the matter as beyond question. But the regulation does not so run. It reads: "If the Secretary of State has reasonable cause to believe. . . . " and thus at once introduces a personal, not an impersonal requirement.

Lord Atkin, in his minority opinion, takes issue with this position and equates the phrase "If the Secretary of State has reasonable cause" with the phrase "If the Secretary of State *thinks* he has reasonable cause." Lord Atkin goes on to argue that the "plain and natural meaning of the words 'has reasonable cause' imports the existence of a fact or state of facts and not the mere belief by the person challenged that the fact or state of facts existed." From this he concludes that the court has the right of jurisdiction in determining the reasonableness implicit in this situation.

Lord Macmillan adds the dimension of the legislative intent that the order in question be applied in war time; therefore, the element of policy obtains weight in his argument. But Lord Atkin, who is no less influenced by policy considerations vis-à-vis the status of the court, states quite categorically,

> In this country, amid the clash of arms, the laws are not silent, but they always speak the same language in war as in peace. . . . In this case I have listened to arguments which might have been addressed acceptably to the Court of King's Bench in the time of Charles I.

Liversidge v. Anderson is cited as a precedent in several cases thereafter, both in England and by judicial systems elsewhere. In *R. v. Secretary of State for Home Affairs ex parte Hosenball* (1977).[4] Lord Denning upholds the majority view of the *Liversidge v. Anderson* case by saying, in no uncertain terms, that

> There is a conflict between the interests of national security on the one hand and the freedom of the individual on the other. The balance between these two is not for a court of law. It is for the Home Secretary. . . . Both during the wars and after them successive ministers have discharged their duties to the *complete satisfaction of the people at large* [italics mine]. . . . They have never interfered with the liberty or the freedom of movement of any individual except where it is absolutely necessary for the safety of the state.

It is perhaps pertinent to remind the reader that we are speaking of reasonableness in this instance as a component of the written law itself, and not reasonableness in the sense of the judge's evaluation of a set of facts. The above-cited judges are all addressing themselves to the question of whether reasonableness is a justiciable issue or not. Is it reasonable by virtue of an independent standard of reasonableness, presumably applied by a court, or is it invariably a personal idiosyncratic standard of the person empowered to use his discretion? This question applies in equal measure to both judicial and executive discretion. The implications of the outcome of the cited cases are such that the court, in determining the nonjusticiability of the reasonableness of the secretary of state's action, is tantamount to saying that the secretary, "acting in good faith," is indeed a reasonable man. This involuted form of reasoning is perhaps a far cry from the Cheyenne and the Barotse, but surprisingly enough the overall result is the same. *Liversidge v. Anderson* is not a clear-cut case to be decided by the application of a valid rule.

The incorporation of the factor of reasonableness into the arguments of the legal realists gives rise to a particular set of problems, the solutions to which are either nonexistent or impractical in everyday judicial decision making. The overall question remains, "What is a reasonable judge?" rather than "What is a reasonable man?" Dworkin provides a partial rescue attempt in his article entitled "Hard Cases." For it is specifically in hard cases that the judge has to choose between alternatives by means of the application of his skill or craftsmanship. If craftsmanship is, indeed, one of the hallmarks of a judge's work, then reasonableness is part of that craftsmanship, just as legal-scientific technique is characteristic of the judge's skill. The point is not lost when Dworkin calls his ideal-type judge Hercules. Given that the source of any law is a political decision, the judge can argue either that the "decision advances or protects some collective goal of the community as a whole," or that the "decision respects or secures some individual or group right" (1975:1059). The former is an argument of policy, whereas the latter is an argument of principle. Following this, a second important distinction is made by Dworkin: the difference between what he terms *background rights* and *institutional rights*. Background rights are "rights that provide a justification for political decisions by society in the abstract, and institutional rights . . . provide a justification for a decision by some particular and specified political institution" (1975:1069–70). The judge, in balancing between these two sets of rights, is placing his own standards of reasonableness to the test.

Dworkin has correctly argued that in hard cases, judges "make use of standards that do not function as rules, but operate differently as principles, policies and other sorts of standards" (1977: 43). In *Liversidge v. Anderson*, the majority opinion of the court appears to be saying that in time of war, considerations of national security outweigh individual liberties. There are rules protecting individual liberties and there are rules protecting national security. There is no rule, however, that categorically states that national security considerations outweigh individual liberties. The judges, therefore, in deliberating on the reasonableness of the actions of the Secretary of State, are adopting policies as guidelines in determining what is, and what is not, reasonable under the circumstances. If a rule is not being applied (although the outcome becomes a precedent for future cases), we can legitimately judge the judges (in terms of our own idiosyncratic policy convictions) as to whether they acted reasonably or not. The positivists may well claim that when the judges bring "nonrule" arguments into their decision making, they are still clearly within the boundaries of legal science, since all they are really doing is interpreting the policy underlying the rule, namely the legislative intent of that rule.

But Dworkin argues beyond this, since not only policy operates as a nonrule factor, but so also does the element of principle. In "Hard Cases" Dworkin provides us with the hypothetical issue of a chess player smiling at his opponent in such a way that may be construed as an attempt to unnerve him. Does this constitute the breach of a rule of chess? Obviously not. If, however, an appeal is made to the referee by the party that considers itself to be injured by the smiling, on what basis can he render a decision? Dworkin seems to find the answer in the institutionalized principles underlying the game of chess, which could be viewed as an intellectual exercise, as opposed to, say, the legitimacy of using psychological intimidation in a game like poker. Returning to Dworkin's distinction between background and institutional rights, the former are abstract entities conforming, perhaps, to general standards of morality, while the latter are expressed as concrete rights. Dworkin goes on to claim that judges arrive at their decisions "by confirming or denying concrete rights" (1975:1078). This distinction is quite convincing. Dworkin rightly asserts that no one can claim an institutional right, which in the case of the chess game is the right to win, by direct appeal to general morality. The bottom line of Dworkin's argument vis-à-vis the chess game is, "given that chess is an intellectual game of some sort, what follows about *reasonable* behavior in a chess game?" (1975:1080, italics mine). From this question Dworkin deduces the following parameters of reasonableness:

> But if the decision in a hard case must be a decision about the rights of the parties, then an official's reason for that judgment must be the sort of reason that justifies recognizing or denying a right. He must bring to his decision a general theory of why, in the case of his institution, the rules create or destroy any rights at all, and he must show what decision that general theory requires in the hard case. (1975:1082)

At this point it might be appropriate to return to Gluckman's reasonable man proposition, and to ask whether Barotse legal reasoning differs from what Dworkin is advocating, or to what extent it constitutes a primitive version of Dworkin's advocacy.

The Barotse are using a two-tiered standard of reasonableness. Their use of the term of the stereotypic "upright man" reflects the generalized morality that would approximate Dworkin's background rights. The Barotse judges, however, do not use this concept in their legal reasonings but refer rather to the specifics of given situations, defined by the "good husband," the "good fisherman," the "good councillor," and so on. The reasonableness of behavior in these roles is determined by the judge's rudimentary consideration of rules, policy, and institutional principles. The Barotse "hard case" cited in chapter 2, in which the judges' verdict determined that the child of an adulterine union belonged to the biological (though irresponsible) father, exemplifies the Barotse attention to institutional rights in clear distinction to the background rights. Although grounds of morality there appeared to be a general recognition that the child would be better off with its sociological father, the Barotse *kuta* nonetheless declared, "It is hard, but is the law: a child must go to its father." From this one may surmise an apparent awareness on the part of the judges that the social implications of the question of paternity override the moral considerations. These implications include the principle that determines the jural rights and legal status of children as a function of paternity in Barotse society. Any contrary decision might have had serious effects on Barotse social structure. If this interpretation is correct, then perhaps even Dworkin might approve of the legal reasoning in this instance by the Herculean Barotse judges.

There are, obviously, many loose ends to be tied up in this chapter, which has meandered through two different schools of legal realism to conclude with the ideas of Dworkin, while also citing cases from both the House of Lords and the Barotse *kuta*. On face value, this might appear to be a somewhat bizarre endeavor, but the sundry elements do assume some kind of shape when they are connected by the conceptual linkage of the idea of reasonableness. If the law is "what the courts do," then the frequency of the use of the term *reasonable* in the reasonings of contemporary Anglo-American courts is an indicator of its relative importance in the judicial process. This point will be developed further in chapter 5. It is sufficient to note, at this stage, that when the application of the appropriate rule is in doubt, there is a tendency toward the judge applying the test of reasonableness to the facts of the case and the behavior of the parties. Ideally, this should be done within the constraints of the authoritative framework of the law, as indicated by Llewellyn and spelled out, albeit differently from Llewellyn, by Dworkin. But more often than not, the craft of judging is reduced to the idiosyncracies of individual judges, who declare that something is reasonable or not without necessarily clarifying the reasons for the mere assertion. Reasonableness often assumes the guise of a permissible escape clause that enables judges in everyday practice to arrive at a decision. One may partially attribute any haphazardness in the recourse to the concept of reasonableness to the degree of professional competency of the judges themselves. Despite the aura and mystique of the virtual infallibility of the judiciary, as perceived by the public at large, judges are no less subject to the variable standards of professional competency as would be applied in any profession.

If legal realism, in its critical capacity, makes a useful contribution, it is in its dimunition of the pretence that law is a science. Harris makes the point that "when legal science speaks of law it does not refer, directly, to the psychological lives of the citizenry" (1980:101). If legal realism succeeds, however, in casting doubt on the actual existence of a legal science, then the "psychological lives of the citizenry" may indeed become a factor of some importance in our understanding of what the law is. In order to forestall any criticism that this implies the logical fallacy of reductionism, the argument is cut off at the point where social and cultural factors condition the "psychological lives of the citizenry." In other words, a legal system is only meaningful in the specific social and cultural milieu within which it operates. The following chapter will address the comparative status of law in so-called utopian communities, specifically in the Israeli kibbutz movement and in some of the communes founded in America during the nineteenth century.

Notes

1. The founding fathers of the Scandinavian school were Hagerstrom and Lundstedt, succeeded by a second generation, Olivecrona and Ross. Hagerstrom, undoubtedly the more influential insofar as legal thought was concerned, was influenced by both Kant and Marx. Hagerstrom

was conforming with the former, when attacking the "will-theory" of law, by positing that the will of the sovereign is an unreal entity, just as by the same token, values have no objective standing. Hagerstrom apparently accepts Marx's idea that law merely masks the raw and blatant use of power on the grounds of implying legitimacy on the psychological assumption that the law "must" be right. All members of the Scandinavian school were skeptics, who attacked what they saw as the "metaphysical" in the theories of others.

2. Hart's definition of these two types of rule is as follows: "Under rules of the one type, which may well be considered the basic or primary type, human beings are required to do or abstain from certain activities, whether they wish or not. Rules of the other type are in a sense parasitic upon or secondary to the first; for they provide that human beings may by doing or saying certain things introduce new rules of the primary type, extinguish or modify old ones, or in various ways determine their incidence or control their operations. Rules of the first type impose duties; rules of the second type confer powers, public or private" (1961:78–79).
3. The issue of *Liversidge v. Anderson* is described in the case summary as follows: "Where the Secretary of State, acting in good faith under reg. 18B of the Defence (General) Regulations, 1939, makes an order in which he recites that he has reasonable cause to believe a person to be of hostile associations and that by reason thereof it is necessary to exercise control over him and directs that that person be detained, a court of law cannot inquire whether in fact the Secretary of State had reasonable grounds in his belief. The matter is one for the executive discretion of the Secretary of State. Therefore, in an action by a person detained against the Secretary of State for damages for false imprisonment the court cannot compel the defendant to give particulars of the grounds on which he had reasonable cause to believe the plaintiff to be a person of hostile associations or that by reason of such hostile associations it was necessary to exercise control over the plaintiff. The production by the Secretary of State of an order of detention, made by him and ex facie regular and duly authenticated, constitutes a defence for such action unless the plaintiff discharges the burden of establishing that the order is invalid."
4. In this case an American journalist had received a deportation order under the Immigration Act of 1971 on the grounds that the home secretary had decided he was a security risk. The court of appeals upheld the home secretary's decision, despite the contention that there had been a breach of rules of natural justice when the home secretary had not disclosed his reasons for the original deportation order.

4

Shared Understandings, Reasonableness, and Intentional Societies

There are shared understandings between members of all socially organized groups. It clearly makes a difference, if, on the one hand, the shared understandings are formally enunciated or plainly stated, and on the other, if they remain in an unenunciated form in the sense of Llewellyn and Hoebel's "felt" norms. Honoré has defined a shared understanding as that in which each member of the group must understand "what the others profess to regard as the proper thing to be done in given conditions" (1973:4). I prefer to substitute *reasonable* in place of *proper*, not merely out of the practical consideration that reasonableness is the subject matter of the present work, but because *proper* signifies an ideal set of expectations, whereas *reasonable* has the attribute of encompassing both ideal and real expectations. Honoré goes on to make another point, which is well taken and will serve to further the argument in this chapter, when he says that "the understanding must relate to a prescription. No prescription is necessary to tell people to do as they please. Natural liberty is the state of affairs existing in the absence of prescriptions. The understanding must relate to something which involves a curtailment of liberty" (1973:6).

In considering those voluntary associations of people who came together in order to create "better" societies, the shared understandings of the membership were clearly understood within the context of the ideological orientations that had originally brought these people together. Certainly, the initial emphasis was on ideally stated, *proper* patterns of behavior. But as time passed, these communities had to make pragmatic readjustments to the wider social and cultural milieu. As commitment to the original ideological precepts waned, the tests of reasonableness also watered down some of the original doctrines. As more and more infractions of the latter took place, the ideological rigidity of the original shared understandings, or the felt norms, was transposed into something different, that of clearly enunciated norms and rules. This was the antithesis of what many of these societies had hoped to achieve—what Karl Marx called "the withering away of the law."

The point of departure in this chapter concerns the Israeli kibbutz movement, which has survived for almost eighty years in its original organizational format. The following account of the kibbutz is based on field research done by me during 1979 and 1980, and published in part in 1981 (Saltman, 1981). Some of the findings of that study are summarized here in order to advance the argument contained in the present work.

The prototype of the kibbutz, known as the *kvutza* (group), was founded at Degania in 1910. Its founding members came together on the basis of an ideology synthesized out of various currents of nineteenth-century Eastern European social thought: ideas of Kropotkin and Bakunin, the naturalism and idealism of Tolstoy, and the social radicalism espoused in the Russian Revolution of 1905. This initial group may perhaps be best described, in Schmalenbach's terms, as a *bund* (1961). This means that the founders came together voluntarily on the basis of an almost mystical communion among themselves that demanded absolute commitment to the shared values of the group. This feature was fairly similar to that which characterized the early stages of some of the American communes. Whereas many of the American communes based their association on the commitment to schismatic doctrines of existing Christian faith, the original "mystical communion" of the kibbutz was purely secular in its orientation. But this could not persist over any length of time. If the first members of Degania saw themselves as members of a single family, the incompatibility between such an organizational principle and the emergence of a biological second generation soon became self-evident. Pragmatic compromises had to be made in order to reconcile the familial values of the collective whole on the one hand and the emerging nuclear families on the other. So what had been the original *bund* soon assumed the form, described by Toennies as a *gemeinschaft*[1].

The kibbutz has maintained the basic format of its organizational structure and functions from the very beginning. Property and the products of labor are owned exclusively by the commune. The individual member contributes his labor, and the kibbutz organizes that labor and redistributes to the membership its combined product in kind, and on an egalitarian basis. Politically, the kibbutz functions as a direct democracy, all members having equal voting rights in the general assembly, which is the sovereign body performing both legislative and judicial functions. It is also the general assembly that elects executive functionaries and committees, which implement the assembly's decisions[2].

Even though the general assembly has always been the sovereign body in each individual kibbutz, it does not reflect the usual characteristics of sovereignty found in other polities. From the outset, the kibbutz gave expression to an antilaw ideology, or, at the very least, a profound distrust in the existence of laws. This position was fairly close ideologically to the thinking in the early years of Soviet jurisprudence. One of the latter's outstanding protagonists, Pashukanis[3], envisaged that the future communist society meant "not the victory of socialist law, but the victory of socialism over any law. . . . Public law is a bourgeois ideological weapon having its highest development under capitalism" (1951:127–29). This basic idea was echoed in the deliberations of the kibbutz founders when they met at Tel Yosef in 1924 to debate a draft of proposed Articles of Association. Shapiro, who has researched the historical data in this instance, quotes one of the speakers at that meeting.

> We have a certain natural opposition to the law. Our taste is to be beyond the framework of laws, and *that* is pleasant for us; for strong in us is the impression of law in capitalist society, law that exists in absolute contradiction to the feeling of justice we have inside us. And through opposition to the existing society we have transferred part of our hatred to law as such. . . . Many of the values most precious to us we have acquired only because we threw off the yoke of the accepted law. (1976:420)

Certainly the lowest common denominator, recognized by both Pashukanis and the kibbutz founders, was that law as an ideology did not represent the interests of the proletariat. Had there been any expectations that the law would simply "wither away" over time, they were not met either in the kibbutz or in the Soviet Union, even though the subsequent directions taken in each instance were quite different.

The nature of law, as such, in the kibbutz, derives in part from the ideological principle underlying the allocation of resources. In addition to the kibbutz having nullified the private ownership of property, kibbutz distributive justice is ideally linked to Marx's dictum, "From each according to his ability to each according to his needs" (Marx, 1875, 1955). The implications of this dictum for legal thinking are significant, especially when if is contrasted with a statement that would supply a utilitarian linkage between the two phrases in Marx's statement. Any utilitarian principle of allocation (for example, "to each in accordance to his contribution") would lend itself well to the formation of formal legal categories that would govern the allocation of resources. Under these circumstances there would be differentially treated classes of persons, things, and actions. Hart has emphasized the generality of these classifications made by the law when he states that the classifications are the essential basis for any kind of formal legal system (1961:121). But the Marxist principle, as adopted and later adapted by the kibbutz, does not lend itself easily to the formulation of categories and corresponding enactments. A rule to the effect that all persons will work for eight hours a day is untenable, since not all persons may be capable of so doing. This accords perfectly with the notion of "from each according to his ability." It is equally meaningless to decree, for example, that all persons with seniority over fifteen years will have television sets in their homes, since it is not beyond the realm of possibility that someone may not want to have a television set in his or her home. In other words, it might not accord to their needs. Given the absence of any utilitarian function linking labor output to the allocation of resources, there remain only generalized norms defining such things as work loads and overall principles of resource allocation.

It is here that reasonableness plays an important role in determining the nature of the two functions, primarily in terms of the leeways afforded by the shared understandings. Individualism is certainly a factor to be reckoned with in the kibbutz context. In a situation wherein precedent counts for very little, reasonableness achieves its full expression. For if in theory all resources are distributed equally, then there is no need for precedents. Shapiro (1976) has used a term, "individualized generality," which on face value appears to be self-contradictory, yet serves to clarify the apparent inconsistencies in the "legal" thinking of kibbutz members. It means that while there are norms defining the general scope of activities within all domains of kibbutz life, the individuality of the members has to be taken into account. The only way this can be achieved, without establishing rigid precedents, is by determining the leeways on either side of the norm in such a way that the outcome would satisfy the tests of reasonableness as understood by all the members of the group.

If the kibbutz has to strike a balance between the generalized norms and the satisfaction of individual requirements, the problems become manifest when an individual finds himself in a state of confrontation either with the community or with another individual. The resolution of the issue is not achieved by reference to an abstract configuration of rights and duties (namely rules). Kamenka and Tay, writing on law in *gemeinschaft*-type societies, state that the litigant appears as "a whole man, bringing with him his status, his occupation and his environment, all of his history and social relationships" (1975:136). The general assembly of the kibbutz, in its judicial capacity, is as much judging the person as it is judging the specific act of behavior that had brought the individual into a state of confrontation. The following cases will illustrate this point.

X, who had been disabled in the 1948 War of Independence, was not a popular member of the kibbutz. It was felt by other members that over the years, X had not been pulling his weight sufficiently in the kibbutz, despite his disability. In addition to this, it was also generally recognized that he was particularly disagreeable in his social relationships with other people. His overall social standing in the kibbutz could be described as low. When, a number of years ago, he had left the kibbutz voluntarily, nobody had been particularly upset about it. After ten years of having lived outside the kibbutz, his wife died and he reapplied for membership. The kibbutz, taking into account his heroism during the war, the fact that his wife had just died, and his sincere professions of commitment to the kibbutz way of life, reaccepted him. But during the following years he did little toward improving his status within the community. It was then discovered that X had been receiving a disability allowance from the Ministry of Defence over the years, which he had been using to pay off his debts from the ten-year period he had lived outside the kibbutz. Furthermore, he was also using this income to help purchase an apartment for his daughter, who lived outside the kibbutz. The generalized norm, perhaps the most basic norm for the kibbutz's *raison d'être*, is that it is forbidden to own private property, which includes income from any source[4]. It was widely assumed that he had been collecting his disability allowance even prior to his having left the kibbutz years ago. The matter was brought before the kibbutz secretariat, which saw no alternative but to bring it before the general assembly. X defended himself by claiming that it was his late wife who had incited him not to declare his private earnings. This was in no way convincing, and several members demanded his expulsion. Some people, however, were bothered by the fact that his second wife was now dying of cancer and that formal expulsion at this stage would be unnecessarily cruel. The situation was perfectly clear to X that he was persona non grata in the kibbutz, and drawing the correct conclusion, he left voluntarily, which was precisely the outcome the kibbutz hoped to achieve. No formal expulsion had been decided upon and no specific statement had been made to the effect that he ought to leave.

Y was a veteran member of the same kibbutz. He was well respected and had "good" social standing. Over the years Y had received substantial reparations from the German government, which he had dutifully transferred to the account of the kibbutz. His daughter had married a young man from abroad and no longer lived on the kibbutz. Given the young couple's financial inability to purchase an apartment in Israel, they were seriously considering a job offer in the United States. Y decided to dock a large portion of the incoming reparations money, remitted to the kibbutz, in favor of his daughter, to enable her to purchase an apartment and not leave the country. In the following months the kibbutz received the reduced income. This was quite intolerable from the point of view of the kibbutz. Y was called before the kibbutz secretariat, which censored his action. But Y remained adamant in his intention to continue assisting his daughter to purchase an apartment. The secretariat suggested that the kibbutz might take on the responsibility of assisting Y's daughter, although this would be at a lower rate of financial support than what the father was presently giving. Y refused on the grounds that this happened to be his personal problem and not the problem of the kibbutz. (This was an inaccurate assessment of the situation by Y.) It became obvious that an impasse had been reached, which could only be broken at the level of the general assembly. While the possibility of expulsion was indeed an option, nobody seriously considered the expulsion of Y as a solution. This was by virtue of his veterancy and his "good" social standing, as well as the peripheral factor of his contribution to the kibbutz, over many years, of the very substantial reparations received from Germany. At the same time, the grounds for expulsion were quite explicit. The basic tenet of not having a private income was being infringed. The general assembly decided to call in an arbitrator from the federated kibbutz movement, with which this kibbutz was associated. The arbitrator, a stranger, found against Y, who was obliged to cease docking sums from the reparations payments but was not obliged to reimburse the considerable sums of money already paid to his daughter during the course of the year. The possibility of expelling Y was not even considered at any stage of the proceedings. Y remained a respected member of the community and continued to serve as a member of several important committees. A number of members of his peer group, however, did react to him thereafter with some reserve, even to the degree of hostility.

The two cases were treated as separate issues, with no linkage of precedent between them. The cases are addressed to the identical issue of an individual member using private income, an act totally antithetical to one of the most basic ideological principles of the kibbutz movement. But it was not the act itself that was being judged, but rather the perpetrators of the act as "whole men," in Kamenka and Tay's meaning of that term. The logic is a far cry from the thinking of a contemporary modern court, which would, first and foremost, look at the act itself. The kibbutz, on the other hand, applies its own tests of reasonableness when addressing itself to the "whole man" concept, establishing identifiable leeways that deviate from the *proper* norms of behavior. In this way, a certain consistency is maintained throughout decision making by means of establishing criteria that define the reasonable or unreasonable kibbutz member.

As long as the shared understandings of the kibbutz were little more than felt norms, and this certainly holds true for the initial stages of the kibbutz's development, the actual standards of reasonableness were widely understood by the whole membership. As the Scandinavian legal realists have suggested, people felt compelled to abide by their ideological commitment to the shared understandings, not so much out of fear of sanctions but rather out of a positive feeling that the self-curtailment of their liberties constituted the proper mode of behavior. These felt norms were not created arbitrarily but were the product of constant ideological discussion and debate. But this type of self-regulating system operates effectively only under conditions of a relatively small-scale population, the members of which are totally committed to a common ideology. The system changes when the group becomes larger and differential gradations of commitment and understanding of the ideological axioms begin to emerge. This latter process is also affected by the nature of the kibbutz's association with the outside world.

Under conditions of increased deviation from the shared understandings, the felt norms gradually become transformed into enunciated norms, in addition to which an incipient set of sanctions begins to materialize. The emergent enunciated norms are not to be construed as laws in any formal sense. They are little more than restatements of what had been previously understood, and as restatements, they bear out Bohannan's contention that some norms are singled out for institutionalization and thus become "customs." The fact that restatement is required is a probable indicator that shared understandings alone are insufficient to prevent deviation. On the highest ideological plane, the kibbutz has clarified for its own purposes Marx's original dictum, "From each according to his ability, to each according to his needs." One of the principal federated movements[5], and perhaps the most ideologically orthodox of the different kibbutz movements—the *Kibbutz Ha'artzi*—

restated the principle at a meeting in Kibbutz Ein Hashophet in 1958:

> The foundations of cooperative life in the kibbutz rest on the principle that each member gives to the society to the best of his ability and the kibbutz cares for the needs of each member *in accordance with its economic ability and the decisions of the movement*. The basic formula of our communal life is indivisible. *Only if* the member gives to the kibbutz to his fullest capacity, *can the ability of the kibbutz to care for the member be guaranteed*. (Kibbutz Ha'artzi Movement: 1964:3, italics mine)

The above quotation is cited from a booklet circulated to all members of the movement by the Department of Social Affairs of Kibbutz Ha'artzi. It is divided into sections and subsections and while many of the paragraphs are based on decisions taken by the movement, the compendium as such has no intrinsic legal standing and is not binding on the individual kibbutzim within the federated movement, nor on their membership. Its stated function is to provide guidelines for the individual members regarding their own activities as well as to help them make decisions over the various spheres of activities within the kibbutz context. Many of the sections implicitly qualify the two clauses of Marx's formula. The issue of the member's contribution to the collective is less complex than those sections that define what the kibbutz allocates to its members. The former describes a normal workload, conditions for working overtime, working on Saturdays and holidays, duty rosters, vacations, and reduced workloads for older members and women after childbirth. All of these are descriptive passages, and there is no mention of sanctions in the event that any of these norms are contravened.

The sections referring to the allocation of resources are also descriptive in their formulation. Basic commodities, such as food and clothing, are distributed on an egalitarian basis, while taking into account the principle of "individualized generality." For example, the issue of clothing is dealt with as follows:

> (i) All clothing requirements of the member will be met in the framework of the budget and with maximal regard to the desire and taste of the member. Within different kinds of categories of clothes, deter-

mined by the department of the Kibbutz Ha'artzi, the member can express his preference for a given item as opposed to another on the basis of norms determined by the movement.

(ii) The Council expresses its opposition to a personal clothing allowance, either in money or in credit points. In order to supply the special needs of members, the budget of the clothing store and the clothing committee may be augmented.

(iii) The kibbutz may elect a clothing committee, the function of which is to clarify and decide upon special problems, demands or enquiries, as well as to ensure the maintenance of the professional abilities of the (clothing store) staff.

The reformulation of the original Marxist precept also had to take into account the existence of commodities under conditions wherein either the demand exceeded the supply or where there was a significant difference in quality of the nature of the commodity (e.g., quality of housing and furniture, high rate of demand for higher education and vacations abroad). All of these are usually distributed unequally on a short-term basis, but in the long run parity is achieved. For example, the distribution of several of these types of articles or privileges may be governed by a waiting list based on the relative chronological seniority of the members.

None of the aforementioned areas of allocation are particularly problematic. They are common knowledge to all kibbutz members; the consensus around them is fairly solid, and since there are rarely "hard cases" on these issues, they are described in a most matter-of-fact style. In turning, however, to those domains that have produced hard cases in recent years, the formulation of the relevant passages is transformed from the straightforward description of norms into what might be considered, in Hart's terminology, as "primary rules of obligation" (1961:79–88). These take the form of either prescriptions specifying what has to be done or clearly stated prohibitions. Regarding the cases cited earlier in this chapter, the relevant section in the compendium concerns property from outside sources.

(i) All property received by a member from outside sources, such as inheritances, payments for artistic and literary creations, reparations, etc., is the sole property of the kibbutz.

(ii) The member is not allowed to ensure for himself an income by means of additional work in any sphere.

(iii) The member is not allowed to waive his rights over family property (i.e., inheritance from non-kibbutz relative) to the benefit relatives living outside the kibbutz. This property belongs to the kibbutz, and the member is obligated to claim it and transfer it to the kibbutz.

It should be noted that even if the norm is clearly enunciated in these paragraphs, it is still little more than the expression of a reasonable shared understanding and does not constitute a *law* in any sense, since it lacks the component of an applicable sanction. Even as an enunciated standard of reasonableness, it is by itself insufficient for the resolution of disputes. In referring back to the two cases mentioned, the determination of the outcome in each case was not achieved by straightforward reference to the stated norm. Quite the contrary; the cases indicated that an additional standard of reasonableness was pitted against the norm itself, that of the differentially qualitative status of the member involved. The leeways afforded, by what Shapiro has termed "individualized generality," provide a basis for consistency, of a sort, in the kibbutz legal culture.

Only under very special circumstances has the kibbutz formulated true, lawlike statements. The relevant domains, for which this holds true, are both specific and highly problematical for the kibbutz. They cannot be handled by the particularistic logic of individualized generality as detailed above. One example of this is the relatively recent problem of drug abuse that has arisen in the kibbutzim. Kibbutz M responded in the following way to a situation in which at least thirty of its members and high-school students admitted to having used drugs of one kind or another on at least one occasion. The preamble to the document condemns the use of drugs as being antithetical to kibbutz way of life. The next section refers to a five-man committee elected by the general assembly, describing its investigative and judicial functions. The following paragraphs contain the main body of the "law":

(i) A member, who is found involved in the use of drugs, will be summoned before the committee and his membership will be suspend-

> ed. The member will be required to cooperate and receive treatment at the discretion of the committee in consultation with professional advisers. After the lapse of one year from the time of the decision, it will be decided whether the person will be readmitted to membership.
>
> (ii) A member found involved in the growing, manufacturing or supply of drugs or found encouraging the involvement of kibbutz youth in drug usage will be expelled from the kibbutz.
>
> (iii) A member who, despite measures taken against him, continues to take drugs or returns to taking drugs, will be expelled from the kibbutz.

As indicated both here and in other references in the text, the only formal coercive sanction at the disposal of the kibbutz is expulsion or temporary suspension of membership. Although there are no published statistics, official or otherwise, relating to the frequency of the application of this sanction, it is widely known that the overall incidence is rare. The claims of the Scandinavian legal realists, as detailed in the previous chapter, would apparently obtain some substance from the kibbutz experience. In other words, it would seem that most people are abiding by the shared understandings, not out of fear of coercive sanctions but presumably as an outcome of some inner compulsion to maintain the standards of those understandings. Unfortunately, it is not quite as simple as that. For, indeed, there exists a set of sanctions that might be appropriately called "informal" sanctions. These are undoubtedly qualitatively different from what is understood as a sanction in the modern legal context of a court of law. Just as there are shared understandings about the expected normative behavior of kibbutz members, so are there shared understandings about what should be done to those who deviate from the norms. The informal sanction lacks the characteristics of a regular legal sanction, one of the more important reasons for this being that the informal sanction remains unenunciated.

Within the kibbutz there are variable degrees of public opinion that can be mustered against a wrongdoer, which can also take a variety of forms. The exercise of public opinion, as a reaction to a member's deviation, is not an arbitrary process. It is extremely well calibrated to the severity of the incident in question, the relative social standing of the member, and the personal sensitivity of the particular member. The effectiveness of public opinion as an informal sanction is to be seen in the progressive escalation of the pressure brought to bear on the offender. The small-scale nature of the society reinforces the efficacy of what is, in its most basic form, a labeling process.

At the lowest level of generating public opinion against a wrongdoer, close relatives and friends may point out in private conversations the wrongness of his attitudes or actions. This was observed to happen in the case of A, who was renowned for his abrasiveness toward everyone with whom he came in contact. Alternatively, we find another mode of pressure applied at this low level—the judicious use of the joking relationship. An older man, B, who in accordance with kibbutz norms was supposed to be working, albeit at a reduced workload, refused to work even at this minimal level. He was constantly subjected to a mild form of teasing by the members of his work group, peer group, and others. In the anthropological literature the joking relationship is often cited as a mechanism for the containment of hostility. Its application in this particular case was effective because the incident itself—the refusal of the old man to work—was not particularly grave; the man in question was sensitive to the reaction, and his veteran standing in the community would not tolerate the application of a severer sanction.

The escalation of sanctions normally involves increasing degrees of social ostracism, ranging from partial to total. An ex-kibbutz member, whose university studies up to the doctoral level had been financed throughout by the kibbutz, showed a growing inclination to embark upon an academic career. This was quite unacceptable to that particular kibbutz. In his own description of the ensuing events, he was subjected to the whole gamut of the different shades of ostracism. This initially involved the proffering of advice by "friendly" mediators, the ever-increasing reserve on the part of his peers in their interaction with him, cessation of mutual visiting, people shying away from vacant seats at his table in the communal dining room, and, at a later stage, people doing their utmost to avoid conversing with him at all. At no point on this continuum of events were the sanctions ever enunciated in any form or by any forum. People just seemed to know what to do and when to do it. When it became absolutely clear that he was not prepared to sacrifice his academic career, he became fully ostracized and left the kibbutz of his own volition.

There is a point beyond the application of nonformal sanctions where public opinion merges with the decision making of the constituted bodies of the kibbutz, be they the kibbutz secretariat, various committees, or in the final instance, the general assembly of the kibbutz acting in its judicial capacity. There are indeed various techniques that have the clear effect of a sanction. If the matter in question is sufficiently serious, or the person in question is blatantly recalcitrant, the kibbutz may choose to publish in its internal newspaper that the person was called before the secretariat for a "clarificatory discussion." This is commonly recognized as a fairly serious move, bridging the gap between the informal and the formal. Other techniques bearing implicit sanction would include the selective placement of the person in different kinds of work situations, some jobs being seen as preferable to others on an internal-prestige ranking scale. Returning to the case of A (the "abrasive" member mentioned earlier), he eventually found himself working as a gardener, which is both solitary and low-prestige work. At a later stage he was relegated to the position of assistant to the woman in charge of the foreign volunteers at the kibbutz, a position that removed him even further from social contact with his fellow members. This arrangement was no less an attempt to arrive at a *modus vivendi* as it was designed to be punitive.

The kibbutz has been singled out for discussion because it emphasizes certain important features of the legal concept of reasonableness. While the common ground of felt norms is present both in the kibbutz and in societies of the Cheyenne type, the parallels cease at this stage of generalized comparison. Kibbutz society is basically a voluntary association, the "culture" of which has been artificially constructed out of an ideology. In comparison, a society such as the Cheyenne is not a voluntary association and its culture is the product of an emergent tradition. This means that the standards of reasonableness employed for judging behavior in the kibbutz are founded on ideological sources, while the equivalent standards among the Cheyenne stem from long-standing cultural tradition. Reasonableness is more manipulatable in the kibbutz context. Mention has already been made of Kamenka and

Tay's notion of the "whole man" being a characteristic judicial standard of *gemeinschaft*-type societies, where matters tend to be judged *ad hominem*. The "whole man" is a close approximation of the "reasonable man." For in societies of this nature, the appeal to reasonableness as a mode for resolving disputes occurs in the absence of clearly defined coercive sanctions. It makes sense that the approach is influenced by *ad hominem* considerations. Furthermore, the kibbutz ambivalence toward law, itself a component of the kibbutz ideology, lends some credence to the importance of reasonableness in the settlement of disputes. But utopian or intentional societies do not exist in a vacuum, just as primitive societies are subjected to modernization. Respective ideologies and traditions undergo radical transformations. As commitment to ideology wanes and traditional values are questioned, the shared understandings shift from unenunciated felt norms to very deliberate sets of statements about how people ought to behave.

A common feature shared by all intentional societies is the declared antipathy toward law in any formal sense of the term. There is an underlying assumption that the *social* predictability, implicit in the ideological self-consciousness of the group, rules out the recourse to *legal* predictability. And what is social predictability? It is merely another term closely related to a variety of terms already cited in this text. It is another way—a functional way—of expressing felt norms, leeways, shared understandings, and mutual expectations, all of which relate to the concept of reasonableness. The one thing they all seem to have in common, above and beyond the intrinsic quality of reasonableness, is the fact that they are not enunciated in any clearly definitive form. Hayek has summed up the significance of this as follows:

> That rules in this sense exist and operate without being explicitly known to those who obey them applies also to many of the rules which govern the actions of man and thereby determine a spontaneous social order. Man certainly does not know all the rules which guide his actions in the sense that he is able to state them in words. At least in primitive societies . . . the structure of social life is determined by rules of social conduct which manifest themselves only by being in fact observed. Only when individual intellects begin to differ to a significant degree will it become necessary to express these rules in a form in

> which they can be communicated and explicitly taught, deviant behaviour corrected and differences of opinion about appropriate behaviour decided. (1973:43)

But it is not only the case of "when individual intellects begin to differ" that the *spontaneous* order meets a challenge. The intellectual differences are themselves only symptomatic of a more fundamental issue. In linking Hayek's concept of the spontaneous order with the idea of social predictability, the main characteristic of the order becomes one of a lack of deliberateness (1973:36). This stands in clear opposition to the idea of legal predictability, where we are dealing with an artificially and deliberately constructed order. Paradoxically, many of the utopian societies, although deliberately established, were nonetheless spontaneous orders. Apart from the ideological principles that brought these communities into existence, the members tended to reject the very notion and implementation of formally constructed rules and laws. Once the ideological principles had been understood and accepted, the members intuitively knew the rules for their behavior, or at the very least, learned them through their interaction with others. One might conclude from Hayek's analysis that as long as the spontaneous arrangements functioned efficiently, the differences between individual intellects were both expressed and contained at the level of ideological debate. But when the spontaneous order could no longer adapt to the impingements of the external environment on the community, the resulting differences of opinion demanded the creation of an order based on legal predictability. For Hayek, the spontaneous order survives only in terms of its ability to maintain a balance with the external environment or by maintaining a cocoonlike existence. In the face of nonadaptibility, the system either creates a rationally devised *made* order or presumably collapses.

The evidence from the kibbutz tends to support Hayek's argument. If the kibbutz began with an antilaw ideology, today it is replete with an ever-increasing corpus of bylaws, and has even produced a parliamentary lobby that advocates special legislation by the Knesset for the kibbutz movement. The kibbutz is not hermetically sealed off from the rest of Israeli society, to which the spontaneous order of the kibbutz must adapt. The wider society is capitalistic and materialistic, and the kibbutz movement interacts with it both economically and politically. Furthermore, the "life style" of the kibbutz has not remained impervious to external influences. The kibbutzim operate sophisticated high-tech industries and have widespread commercial contacts throughout the world. These industries require high-level managerial, engineering, and technical staff, the majority of which has emerged from within the kibbutz movement itself. Many of these individuals also work outside of the kibbutz in a wide variety of positions in the country's public and private sectors.

From the kibbutz's point of view, the influx of foreign volunteers has brought in its wake many alien and undesirable influences upon the younger generation. All of this, together with army service and university studies, has brought the kibbutz movement into the highest frequency of interaction with the outside world than at any time in its history. The problems of kibbutz "leavers" are weighty. Until some thirty years ago, people who left the kibbutz could successfully begin a new life on the outside with little more than the clothes on their backs. This was because the external society at that time was relatively egalitarian in comparison with what obtains now. The dominant middle-class, materialistic values of contemporary Israeli society force the kibbutz leaver to bring his own capital just to survive while making a new start. He leaves the kibbutz, albeit voluntarily, but nonetheless with substantial financial compensation, as sanctioned by national legislation on workmen's compensation.

In this every-growing complexity of relationships with the outside world, the inherent reasonableness of the spontaneous order is severely tested and, in some domains, has proved insufficient for resolving the problems deriving from the kibbutz's interaction with its wider social and cultural milieu. In Hayek's terms, the adaptive response has been the ever-greater reliance on the "made" order. This takes the form of deliberately formulated codes of behavior, designed to protect the more fundamental aspects of the ideology in the face of potentially intrusive damage from external sources.

One of the conclusions has to be that any spontaneous notions of what may have originally constituted standards of reasonableness are, in the long run, fighting a losing battle against the dominant ethos of individualism that has developed in the kibbutz and is reinforced by outside influences. In this respect the intentional societies reflect the same overall trend toward the demise of shared understandings over reasonableness. This point has been reformulated here to mean the transformation from a spontaneous order, based on social predictability, to a made order, based on legal predictability. The former reflects shared but nonenunciated understandings about the standards for reasonable behavior, whereas the latter has to rely on consciously definable and enunciated canons of what is, and what is not, reasonable. The question now becomes twofold: What factors contribute to the decline of the spontaneous order and its perceptions of reasonableness, and what is the effectiveness of the measures, in Hayek's adaptive sense, in combatting this process almost as a rearguard action?

Common to all the socialist communes is the characteristic mechanism of distributory justice, based on the generalized principle, "From each according to his ability, to each according to his needs." Any challenge to this principle arises at the limits of this concept—either people who work less than might be reasonably expected, or those who demand more than what is construed as their reasonable needs. The evidence from the experiences of the nineteenth-century communes seem to indicate that in those instances where a significant number of members did not contribute "according to their ability," the communes in question were short-lived. One of the prime examples of this type of failure was that of the Owenite[6] experiment of the 1820s (Harrison, 1969: 178–79).

Reasonable need was not only emphasized for its importance by the theoreticians of utopianism—Plato, More, Rousseau, and others—but was also realized as such in the practical experience of the commune members themselves. It became an inescapable provision for their communal existence. Reasonable need essentially meant austerity, which admittedly at the inception of a commune's existence was not too hard to achieve, since the resources themselves were meager. Moreover, the social consequences of these circumstances were quite clear. Erasmus has written: "By meeting the same needs for all members and by requiring continual adherence to the limits of reasonableness it defines, collective consumption automatically reinforces the unanimity of group goals and simultaneously makes everyone's devotion to them continually visible to everyone else" (1977:119). But as time passed and the economic surpluses of these communities grew, "reasonable need" could no longer be defined in terms of the relative value of austerity. Consequently, the concept of reasonableness under such conditions was no longer characterized by unanimity and became an issue for debate.

Contention usually took the form of individual goals being pitted against collective goals. In these instances the limits of reasonableness were being put to the test. The reevaluation of current standards of reasonableness in light of the economic status of the community at any given time was only one of a number of strategies employed to face these problems. Other alternatives included the fission of the larger group into separate, smaller communities, the assumption here being that shared understandings are more likely to be maintained as a practical device within the confines of a smaller-scale community. Another outlet was the emergence of a political leadership that was capable of commanding allegiance to the original ideological principles of association and, at the same time, resolving the disputes created by the weakening consensus. In many cases, however, what happened in reality was either the radical transformation of the group into a different organizational structure or, ultimately, the complete dissolution of the community.

The demographic problem with all its social consequences was recognized as such quite early on in the history of the kibbutz movement. By the 1920s the prototypic group at Degania faced the issue by splitting its growing membership and establishing Degania "B". At the time, this act constituted a serious ideological confrontation within the ranks of the kibbutz movement as a whole. The proponents of maintaining limited small-scale groups were very much aware of the relationship between group size and the consensus on shared understandings. The opponents, on the other hand, were motivated by wider economic and nationalistic considerations, and larger kibbutzim were seen viable both as a means for propagating the communal ideal and for achieving political goals in Palestine. The debate between the two groups was often fierce, but after seventy-five years, the outcome of this difference has not been too significant. The average size of a contemporary kibbutz is within the tolerable range of several hundred members. Of the American communes, only the Hutterites kept to a deliberate policy of group fission. "When the population of a Hutterite[7] colony reaches 130 to 150, half of the group moves on to newly acquired lands to form a new Bruderhof, a process called 'branching out'" (Erasmus, 1977:130). It is not really possible to determine an optimum size beyond which the whole fabric of shared understandings and reasonable expectations begin to deteriorate. The knowledge that this occurs is more of a common-sense proposition than an objectively determined fact.

In the face of waning commitment, one of the strategies already noted is the emergence of a political leadership that strives to maintain that commitment. Many of the early American communes were associated with charismatic individuals, who were either the founders of the movements or emerged as leaders during the course of events. The Shaker movement was associated with its founder, Anne Lees, and later with Joseph Meachum. The Rappites took their name from their founder, a separatist Lutheran preacher. The Zoar community was founded and led by Joseph Bimeler, as was the Oneida community by John Noyes. Similarly, the relatively long-lived success of the Amana Society, in its original form, could be attributed to its leader, Christian Metz. The Hutterites, on the other hand, were exceptional in their low-profile leadership, but as already noted, they employed an alternative strategy by keeping their communities small. Nor did the Israeli kibbutz movement produce charismatic leaders at the level of the individual kibbutz, although there has always been a number of prominent ideologues at the national level of the federated kibbutz movements.

Under the differential conditions of direct democracy on the one hand, as represented by the kibbutz, and the often autocratic leadership of such people as Noyes on the other, the concept of reasonableness assumes different forms. Furthermore, many of the nineteenth-century American communes in their capacity of religious foundations also had a distinctive supernatural taint that colored their notions of reasonableness. Under the *ideal* conditions of direct democracy there is, at least in theory, an egalitarian distribution of power. In contrast, the founding spiritual leader of the autocratic type of commune imposed his own notions of reasonableness as a charter for social predictability. Note *social* rather than *legal* predictability, since in most cases the leader did not even bother to codify or systematically lay out the norms in detail. He remained a leader by virtue of his charisma and for as long as his followers chose to accept him as such and be committed to his ideas. But even the secular egalitarian communes share similar problems to those faced by the religious and charismatically led communities. Even if there is no evidence for the emergence of a class structure in this type of community, status differentials are unavoidable. Erasmus, writing on this point, states, "Differences in material goods are much easier for communes than are differences in status and rank. . . . in letting their most capable come to the top, the egalitarian commune must be careful that no symbolization of this status undermines group equality" (1977:140). The leaders of the Rappites, Zoarites, and Oneidans enjoyed higher political status, together with material benefits accruing from that status. The Shakers, Amana Inspirationists, and Hutterites maintained a hierarchical organization, (called a "chain of command" by Erasmus), although no significant privileges or material benefits derived from the status.

The kibbutz has produced its proportionate share of talented leadership, but many of these individuals, although remaining kibbutz members, have been and are siphoned off into the arenas of national politics, the military, the universities, trade unions, and industry. All these domains undoubtedly serve to reduce these people's more active involvement in the local politics of the individual kibbutzim. Status differentials, as already noted, do exist at this level, but the kibbutz has neither institutionalized these differences nor symbolized its elite in any particular way. While structurally the kibbutz still maintains a format of direct democracy, the efficacy of this type of social control is very much a function of the members' willingness to actively participate. In referring specifically to this, Ben-Rafael has pointed out that "this tendency [membership participation] was to weaken over the course of time as the amplification of resources called for increased competence. The result was the gradual emergence of hierarchies covering a wide range of positions both in the work area and in public functions" (1979:91). Despite the weakening of direct democracy as a consequence of less active universal participation, the kibbutz has not opted to substitute representative democracy in its place. Rosner and Cohen have written,

> The favourable attitude toward written regulations, secret ballot and transfer of authority from assembly to committees proves that in spite of the almost unanimous opposition to electing a council of representatives, there is a weakening of the components of the theoretical model of kibbutz democracy. The data can be seen also as a kind of validation of the theoretical model and of our basic assumption on the link between direct kibbutz democracy, ideological commitment (value consensus) and social solidarity (no interest groups and high identification with the kibbutz). In such a situation the outcome of a transition to representative democracy might not be a better adaptation to changing conditions, but might weaken the ideological and social foundations of the kibbutz. (1983:233)

The application of standards of reasonableness to conflict situations characterizes the pragmatic readjustments that the kibbutz had to make in order to protect itself against the onslaught against its communistic ideology both from within and without. Van de Berghe and Peter (1988) made a comparative study of the kibbutz and the Hutterite communities, focusing precisely on this factor of pragmatic readjustment. They emerge with a term, *nepotistic communism*, the implications of which are not too different from the term *individualized generality* as employed previously. Both terms have the same built-in characteristic of contradiction, which emphasizes the nature of the basic problem faced by these communities. They argue that ideological commitment is an insufficient condition for the long-term survival of these communities. They go on to state that "our two cases were successful, not because the ideological commitment of members succeeded in repressing self-interest and nepotism, but because both groups pragmatically modified their ideology to accommodate an irrepressible individualism and familism" (1988:524). Furthermore, "both systems pragmatically evolved a set of creeping compromises that might be termed 'nepotistic communism'" (ibid., 533). Subsequently they also claim that "in respect to nepotism, both groups have in effect made their peace with it. They are reconciled to its inevitability; they recognize it as a constraint on the communal ideal; and they have devised mechanisms to keep it within such bounds as not to threaten the integrity of the larger community" (ibid., 537).

These, then, are the broad parameters within which reasonableness operates. The ideological component of the communal system makes virtually impossible demands on what is, ultimately, the self-seeking individual. Such an individual is in a permanent state of quandary in both assessing the reasonableness of his own actions as well as the actions of others, in the light of the ideological rigidity. If he makes allowances for others, by deeming their actions *not unreasonable*, it is certainly not out of altruism but probably more out of a sense that this is exactly the way he might wish to behave. The leeways are important for the survival of the community, no less than for the survival of each satisfied member of that community. Consequently, behavior is being constantly subjected to the test of reasonableness in a pragmatic endeavor to maintain the balance between conflicting interests.

Pitting deviance against norms as a set of binary oppositions is too simplistic a device to enable us to understand how reasonableness operates effectively in these intentional communities. Shenker's study of intentional communities (1986) reveals the more subtle mechanisms involved. These mechanisms reflect in part the contentions of some of the Scandinavian realists. Shenker suggests, in referring to the Hutterites, that an individual "must act correctly, because he *actively believes* (both words are operative) his actions to be correct" (1986:197). The element of coercion is minimized, and in ascribing the same idea to the kibbutz, Shenker writes, "I suggest that the individual member conforms to the rules, *because he wants to* and that the problem of intentional communities is to *sustain his desire for conformity rather than to prevent deviance*" (ibid., 213).

There is a degree of concurrence between Shenker's conclusions and the findings of the present writer, insofar as both agree that it is not the deviant act of behavior that defines the problem of deviance. It has already been argued that it is the "whole man" who is being subjected to judicial scrutiny rather than the isolated deviant action. Shenker argues his case somewhat differently, and quite convincingly, when he says that "in an intentional community the problem of deviant behaviour is not so much the deviant act itself as the consequence of the act for the sense of commitment in other members" (ibid., 205). It is here that he injects an interesting proposition that provides an additional dimension to the idea of the whole man. For, according to Shenker, deviance is not only "under-conformity" but can also be "over-conformity." In other words, the person who behaves as an ideological purist is no less an irritant to his fellows than the person who blatantly fails to conform. Shenker describes this by asserting that "deviant behaviour is not that which departs from *ideal* standards, but that which departs too much from *accepted* standards" (ibid., 210). Clearly, this is a formula that would be totally unacceptable in a modern court of law. He suggests that the reasons for this are that people would find absolute adherence psychologically difficult to sustain. There would also have to be explicit sanctions for nonadherence. Furthermore, absolute adherence would impede the necessary adaptations to changing circumstances. Thus, breaking the acceptable rules within reasonable leeways is, apparently, a necessary safety valve for the individual's psychological well-being. This is not a reductionist psychological explanation for a social phenomenon, since it refers specifically to the mental state of the individual as a consequence of social pressures. If Shenker is correct, it would appear that reasonableness as a judicial standard plays a very important role in this type of community.

What may have been reasonable to the communes was not necessarily seen in the same way by the nation's courts. Although some verdicts of Israeli courts have challenged ideologically motivated tenets of kibbutz existence, they have been few and their social impact has not been too great. In nineteenth-century America the situation was somewhat different. Some of the social and cultural practices of the communes were perceived by the outside world as bizarre, to say the very least. They became issues for passionately opinionated public debate, and when specific matters were brought before the courts, the judges had little alternative but to address themselves to the substantive issues. A major criterion employed by the courts was whether or not these practices conflicted with principles of public policy. In a number of instances they quite clearly did conflict, particularly given the fact that many of these communities had been established as an expression of ideological revolt against the public policy of their time.

The most contentious issues were those relating to marriage and family. Wherever the "external" law was patently clear, so was the outcome equally clear. The Mormon practice of polygyny brought that community into direct conflict with the standing law on bigamy. The principle of freedom of religious practice, as guaranteed by the Constitution, was an insufficient defense. This was established in the case of *Reynolds v. United States* (1878), in which the Supreme Court was not sparing in its language when it referred to the Mormon practice as "odious," and on a subsequent occasion, *Mormon Church v. United States* (1890) described it as a "return to barbarism." In the case of *Davis v. Beason* (1890) the Supreme Court said quite categorically that bigamy and polygamy were crimes that "tend to destroy the purity of the marriage relation, to disturb the peace of families, to degrade women and to debase men. To call the advocacy of plural marriage a tenet of religion is to offend the common sense of mankind" (Weisbrod, 1980:21). As a social comment, this goes far beyond the judicial canons of reasonableness and the criteria for the determination of legality.

In other cases the courts found fit not only to deem the communes' behavior unreasonable but to go as far as to question the sanity of the behavior. Weisbrod (ibid., 55) summarizes the case of *State ex rel. Stephen Ball v. Anna Hand* (1848). Ball, on the death of his wife, left his children in the care of his mother. On subsequently joining the Shaker community, he sued for the custody of his children. The grounds were clear that a natural parent has a greater claim for custody than a grandparent, but the judge thought otherwise. In ruling against the father, the judge stipulated,

> He seeks them that he may sever them from the bosom of their grandmother and from his own bosom, and plant them in the cold ascetic bosoms of the "female caretakers". . . . this may be done by an honest man, and a pure man. But can it be done by a sane man? Does it not argue, at least, a morbid state of the amative and philoprogenitive faculties, bordering on insanity and totally inconsistent with a rational discharge of parental duty?

The judge's legal rationale was anchored in a statutory prescription to the effect that if the father were to be found "grossly immoral, intemperate, imbecile, insane or otherwise disqualified to discharge the obligation of providing," he did not have the right of custody of his children.

But if the internal mores of the communes were often found wanting in several respects by the courts, not so were the overall contractual relationships between a member and the commune.

The period was characterized by the laissez-faire ideology that reigned supreme in the economic and political life of the United States. The legal concept of "freedom of contract" provided the communes with more than adequate protection against dissenters and seceders who brought suits against the communes. If consenting adults had voluntarily ceded their property to the communes and, thereafter, sought to recover through recourse to the courts, they found little in the way of relief by this approach. It made little difference if they presented evidence to demonstrate the most bizarre features of the communal life or the dictatorial habits of the commune leaders, even proving the existence of servitude. Public policy of the time was laissez-faire. It was too sacrosanct a notion to be challenged by a substantive evaluation of the reasonableness of the contractual relationship.

This indicates that reasonableness in a formal legal context is employed in a very different way than has been depicted for the internal arrangements of the intentional communities. The emergent picture has been one of communities that owe their survival, in no small measure, to the idea of reasonableness. Throughout this text reasonableness has been synonymously associated with a variety of other concepts—felt norms, shared understandings, leeways, spontaneous orders, and the whole man. These are all subjective categories given to the influence of cultural relativity, group consciousness, and even individual understandings. They have no place in a logically constructed system, which is perceived by its practitioners as being governed solely by objective criteria. The next chapter will examine the use of the concept of reasonableness in the contemporary courts applying English law.

Notes

1. Toennies made a distinction between two forms of society—the *gemeinschaft*, which is a communal society, and the *gesellschaft*, which is an associational society. In the former it is the overall communal interest that bonds people together. In contrast, one of the major characteristics of the *gesellschaft*-type society is the voluntary basis for association that is specifically geared to the rational pursuit of self-interest.
2. The existence of functionaries and committees, of course, ultimately dilutes the element of direct democracy by bureaucratizing decision

making. The general assembly does remain the sovereign body, but its democratic efficacy is a function of the willingness of the members to participate.

3. While it is impossible to summarize Pashukanis's work in a footnote, suffice to point out that one of his main contentions was that law is not basically intrinsic to man's personality, but is rather a legalistic interpretation of man's labor as an exchangeable commodity.
4. Today this norm is being consistently contravened. The high frequency of contravention might indicate tacit acceptance of the phenomenon.
5. Individual kibbutzim are organized in three major national movements, which are in turn linked to political parties in the national sphere. The largest of the three movements, the Takam, is associated with the Labour Alignment party, and is less orthodox in its implementation of the original principles of kibbutz ideology than the Kibbutz Ha'artzi, which is allied to Mapam, a socialist party. The third movement, the Kibbutz Hadati (the religious kibbutz movement), is associated mainly with the major Zionist religious party, the Mafdal.
6. Robert Owen, a British industrialist and philanthropist, established a secular commune that, on the basis of scientific rationalism, would emulate the social and economic achievements of the existing religious communes. Some thousand persons of random origin gathered at Owen's proposed site for the commune in Indiana (named New Harmony), in 1825. The lack of any common ideological or social basis, as well as the chance to live off Owen's subsidy, militated against any successful outcome, and the community disintegrated after two years. Subsequent experiments met with similar failure.
7. The Hutterites' origin is in the Anabaptist movement formed at the time of the Reformation. After considerable relocation of these communities throughout Europe, a number of colonies were established in the United States between 1874 and 1877. The Hutterite movement, living in small, predominantly agricultural communities, known as *Bruderhof*, has survived to the present day.

5

Reasonableness in a Modern Legal System

Reasonableness, as a concept employed in modern legal systems, is both elusive and multifaceted. The word appears in statutes and in precedents. It is written into contracts and wills. It is also an adjective used to qualify other concepts, such as *care, cause, time, maintenance,* and so forth. It is a test employed by judges, on occasions, to evaluate facts submitted to lower-level courts, yet it has different connotations at the level of appellate courts, which deal primarily with rulings on matters of law. As will be pointed out, there is no necessary equivalence between "reasonableness" and "legality." This is quite an important distinction, since the mental processes involved in arriving at a conclusion are clearly different from those employed in making an assessment as to what may be reasonable. Reasonableness also assumes different meanings within the contexts of fact finding and rule finding. Yet these are not separate issues, for the findings of superior courts are bound to influence the decision making of the lower tribunals. All of this is a far cry from the shared understandings that underlie reasonableness in some of the other legal cultures already described.

Appellate judges seemingly engage in much semantic casuistry in order to confine themselves to the legality of an issue rather than having to address themselves to the intrinsic reasonableness of the given situation before them. In fact, they tend to resist the attempts of litigants to formulate their cases in the latter mode. In *R. v. Hillingdon London Borough Council ex parte Pulhofer and Another* (judgment given in the House of Lords on 7 February 1986, as reported in the *Times Law Report*) the applicants claimed that the accommodation provided by the council under the Housing (Homeless Persons) Act 1977 was not "appropriate," or not reasonable. The argument was that a "person did not have accommodation within the meaning of the act and was, therefore, 'homeless', if he occupied premises that either were not large enough to accommodate the family unit or lacked the basic amenities of family life; such basic amenities should include not only sleeping but also cooking, washing, and eating facilities." The applicants and their two small children were living in a guest house with no cooking facilities, no eating facilities such as a table and chairs, and with only three bathrooms in the whole building to serve thirty-six persons.

The judges, in dismissing the applicants' plea, made the following argument, to which I have applied the descriptive term, "semantic casuistry." The words *appropriate* or *reasonable* were not to be imported into the terms of the law. Accommodation could only be aptly described within the ordinary meaning of the English language. *Ordinary*, as understood by the judge, is obviously something qualitatively different from *appropriate* or *reasonable*, but the only clue obtained as the judge's train of thought in making this distinction, is to be found in his statement that "it would be a misuse of language to describe Diogenes as having occupied accommodation within the meaning of the 1977 Act." This metaphorical *reductio ad absurdum* does little to clarify the boundaries between *ordinary, reasonable,* and *appropriate*. A less flippant argument for the rejection of the plea, even though somewhat reminiscent of the style of Lewis Carroll, was the judge's assumption of legislative intent—that the Act was "to assist persons who were homeless, not an Act to provide them with homes." The court went on to recognize that the "plight of the applicants in the present case commanded the deepest sympathy." This sympathy, however, was insufficient in the balance to fortify the judge's option in employing his own discretion for monitoring the activities of the local council. He had determined the limits by stating that he would only intervene if it could be shown that the "public body, consciously or unconsciously, was acting perversely." Clearly, from the point of view of this judge, the local council was not acting perversely. But this conclusion was reached without any serious reference to the substantive matter of what might constitute perversity.

So while we know that had the council offered the family in question a barrel for accommodation, the judge would have considered this perverse and, consequently, illegal, we do not know whether the gradations between Diogenes's housing arrangements and what was actually offered—a tent, a shack with a leaking roof, or the same accommodation with only one bathroom for thirty-six persons—would be perverse or not. To achieve a judgment here, the concepts of *ordinary, reasonable,* and *appropriate* would have to merge, and it makes no difference whether the word *reasonable* appears in the text of the statute or not. It is also insufficient to argue that each case would have to be treated as a discrete issue and be decided on its own merits. The case cited here bears the same open-ended characteristics of Hart's conundrum, "There will be no vehicles in the park." Does this cover roller skates or an airplane passing through the park's airspace? If the definition of the phenomenon is at the discretion of the judge, he can only fall back on reasonableness as a standard in making his decision. For all intents and purposes, the judge in this case, by avoiding the actual issue of whether the accommodation was reasonable or not, was in fact determining that it was legal because it was not perverse. He was also determining in this case that there is no necessary equivalence between reasonable and legal. In order to achieve this outcome, the judge is pairing off words into sets of binary oppositions throughout his argument—ordinary/reasonable, ordinary/perverse, perverse/legal, and legal/reasonable. The argument is an abstract game of words, in which the judge has the option of choosing which words will stand in opposition to each other. The implicit critical undertones in the description of this case are only critical from the standpoint of a sociologist or a semanticist. From a lawyer's point of view the decision is valid, since the terms of the relevant statute did not require the judge to consider the reasonableness or the appropriateness of the accommodation.

Where the word *reasonable* is actually written into the text of the statute, even appellate judges are under a constraint to consider the matter. The apparent tendency, however, is that higher courts will accept the decisions of lower courts, other tribunals, bodies, or persons having the authority to determine what constitutes reasonableness, so long as the procedures are legitimate. The underlying assumption is that not only do these bodies have the authority to arrive at these decisions, but they also have the competency to do so. Furthermore, there is a reluctance on the part of the judiciary to become involved in matters that may have far-reaching political implications. This could bring the judiciary into potential conflict with the legislative and executive branches of government, as well as arousing controversy in the arena of public opinion. The legal system, as well as the other branches of government, is sensitive to public opinion, albeit for different reasons. But despite this reluctance, there are occasions on which these issues cannot be avoided.

Different judges, at various times, have determined criteria whereby the court will exercise its discretion in examining the substantive issue, and may even overturn executive or lower-court decisions. Since these criteria tend to be variations on basic ideas, it is sufficient to cite one such set of criteria as an example. Wade (1971:70–88) cites the example by reference to the case of *Associated Picture Houses Ltd. v. Wednesbury Corp.* (1948). In this case the local authority granted a licence for a cinema to open on Sundays, on condition that children under the age of fifteen be barred from admission. The Cinematographic Act of 1909 stated quite clearly that the opening of cinemas on Sundays was "subject to such conditions as the authority thinks fit to impose." The Master of the Rolls, Lord Greene, presented the classic argument that the courts can only intervene in an executive decision when that decision is shown to be illegal. He then goes on to provide four parameters of motivation that the court would have to take into account in exercising its discretion to intervene or not. "Bad faith" and "dishonesty" require no further elaboration. But the other two parameters—"*unreasonableness*" and "*disregard of public policy*"—are problematic. Since the present case was brought on the grounds that the decision of the local council was both *ultra vires*[1] and unreasonable, was the court under any obligation to consider the substantive issue? Lord Greene's argument is in the negative. The only question to be considered was whether the local authority behaved reasonably in arriving at its decision. Lord Greene considered that the local authority had the competency to decide on the "well-being and the physical and moral health of children." He finalized his argument by pointing out the distinction between what the court might have thought about the reasonableness of the local authority's decision and the question of whether the local council had acted reasonably.

There is an element of tautology in Lord Greene's test for reasonableness. Executive discretion must be exercised reasonably "in the sense that it must not be so unreasonable that no reasonable authority could have reached it." The phrasing in the double negative is presumably intentional, obfuscating, of course, what might be construed as reasonable or not. This sentence may also help to understand how the judge in *R. v. Hillingdon London Borough Council* (sup.) imported the word "perverse" into his argument. But it must be remembered that this is a test for reasonableness and not a definition of reasonableness. What is actually meant here? Does it refer to the substance of the actual decision or merely to the reasonableness of the competency of the authority to make such a decision? At the same time, how can one be restricted to the issue of the competency without considering the substance? The distinction that Lord Greene draws between what the court might have thought about the reasonableness of the local authority's decision and the question of whether the local authority acted reasonably is misleading. If Lord Greene only considered that the local authority had competency to decide upon the well-being and physical and moral health of children, it is an evasion of his own test of whether the administrative action might have been so unreasonable that no reasonable authority could have reached it. He employed his test only to evaluate the legitimacy of the local authority's right to make a decision in this domain. It is, of course, impossible to know what Lord Greene's motivation was for this particular course of action: insistence on a formal approach to law or a sympathetic concurrence with the local authority's actual decision. Most lawyers would opt for the former consideration, whereas the nonlegal observer could certainly entertain the suspicion that the latter might have been a prime motivation. Why did Lord Greene choose to classify the "well-being and physical and moral health of children" as falling within the competency of the local authority rather than classifying it as a phenomenon for parental discretion? The contention, stated and restated in this text, is that we are dealing with the reasonableness of the judge, who is empowered or authorized to make the determination regarding what constitutes reasonableness.

Part of the reluctance of judges to deal with issues of reasonableness derives from their insistence on circumscribing their activity to questions of legality, insofar as this is possible. As noted earlier, there is no necessary equivalence between *reasonableness* and *legality*. A case illustrating this point is *Lanarkshire Steel Co. v. Caledonian Railway Co.* (1903). In this case the plaintiffs claimed that the railway company had unreasonably raised its rates, and although they had paid the increased rates under protest, it was understood that they would be allowed a rebate if and when it was proven that the railway company had not been entitled to the increase. The appropriate tribunal for determining the reasonableness of the rates was the railway and canal commissioners, as determined by statute. Seven other companies had filed suit against the unreasonableness of the rate increase, and the commissioners had found in their favor. The judge in the present case held that the findings of the commissioners vis-à-vis the seven other companies also applied to the plaintiffs. But in the present case the plaintiffs were sueing for damages in their attempt to recover the sum of money they had paid under protest. In order to recover in a suit for damages, the plaintiffs would have to prove before the court that the rate increase was illegal, and unreasonableness is an insufficient ground for that purpose. The judge pointed out that *unreasonable* and *illegal* are not synonymous, and it is the court's duty to determine what is legal. The railway commissioners' decision (that the increased charges could not be made because they were unreasonable) could not have been made by a court, unless the court was under a statutory obligation to do so. Even though the railway commissioners had determined that the charges were unreasonable, this does not mean that "there was any antecedent illegality in charging it." The judge went on to determine that the recovery of the excess charges paid by the plaintiffs is a point of law and not an issue dependent "upon the application of the standard of what is fair and equitable in the circumstances of the particular case." The plaintiffs lost their case.

One can understand the entrenchment of appeals judges concerning the distinction between reasonableness and legality, as well as the basic claim that such courts deal almost exclusively with questions of legality. But even if these highest practitioners of law are committed to the professional practice of legal science, does this imply that they are morally released from the obligation of dispensing that vague commodity known as justice, or at the very least, preventing injustices? There are points beyond which the commitment to professionalism creates situations whereby fairness is ignored and injustices emerge. Members of the legal profession, of course, are fully aware of this. Some of the examples cited here clarify Llewellyn's critique of the formal style of appellate judging in that it lacks what Llewellyn has called "wisdom" and "situation sense." But if appellate judging is directed primarily toward the application of the correct rule (unless specifically directed by statute to do otherwise), the orientation of trial judges is geared toward fact finding and the assessment of these facts.

An example of detailed and painstaking reasoning in this context is found in *Perry v. Ellis* (1946). The plaintiff was struck from behind and injured by the defendant, who was driving his car. It was dark and misty at the time of the accident and the road was poorly lit. It was established that the defendant was driving at a reasonable speed in light of the prevailing conditions, and that his headlights were operating efficiently. But the windscreen was wiped by a single blade that cleared only a semicircular portion. The plaintiff claimed, among other things, that "the area cleared by the wiper was insufficient to enable the defendant to maintain an efficient lookout, and in the circumstances he was guilty of negligence."

The judge carefully reviewed the reconstruction of the whole sequence of events in considerable detail, and having established the veracity of the facts to his own satisfaction, went on to test them by employing standards of reasonableness. Up to a point, the style is somewhat reminiscent of that of a Barotse judge: The judge in the present case is formulating such questions as what might be expected from reasonable drivers and reasonable pedestrians, casting the reasonable man into defined roles. Unlike the Barotse judge, however, the judge in this case does not use his findings to berate, patronize, or morally educate the litigants before him. He is striving, in practical terms, to arrive at a verdict. But even so, the boundary between Barotse moralizing and the present example of a modern judge's implicit criticism of the litigants' behavior is little more than a thin line. In this case, both litigants are gently chided for their nonfulfilment of obligations in their respective roles. According to the judge, the defendant was "blameworthy in that the state of the windscreen did not permit him to see an object in line with the near side of the motor car. . . . " Although the judge most categorically denied that he was employing a standard of perfection, he went on to argue that

> the shield is provided for comfort and convenience and for the protection of driver and passengers against wind and weather. If its presence involves danger, and there is no other means of overcoming the peril, it should be removed or raised out of the way. Alternatively, the defendant, in the absence of any other convenient means, should have stopped at proper intervals to wipe the glass clear of moisture, thereby enabling him to have a full range of vision.

What the judge did not examine, and presumably could not, were the following questions: What were the conditions on the night of the accident that governed the accumulation of moisture on the windshield? At what rate did it accumulate? Given the rate of the accumulation, what would be a reasonable frequency incumbent upon the driver to stop and wipe the moisture from the windshield? The phrase, "a full range of vision," is the language of perfection. Despite his denial, the judge seems to be aware that he might possibly be using a standard of perfection. This is indicated by his apparent need to cite precedent in order to bolster his argument. The case cited was *Baltimore & Ohio Railroad Co. v. Goodman* (1927), where it was held that "if a driver of a vehicle is about to cross a railway track and he cannot be sure otherwise whether a train is dangerously near, he must stop and get out of the vehicle." The analogy to the circumstances of the present case is surely a weak one.

The judge was even more censorious of the plaintiff. Given the conditions of that night, and given that the plaintiff's hearing was also defective, she had clearly not taken reasonable precautions to prevent the accident. She carried no light, she wore dark clothing, and she did not bother to ascertain the approach of vehicles from behind by looking back to check from time to time. "In the situation in which she had placed herself, she should have omitted no step reasonably prudent to ensure her own safety. . . . She was guilty of negligence that continued up to, and was a proximate cause of, the collision." The judge found for the defendant. The case had been argued throughout, both on the basis of fact finding and the application of qualitative standards, in order to assess the facts. The judge was little concerned with rule finding, although thirteen cases were cited by counsel, another thirteen cases were referred to by the judge, and there were two references to the Road Traffic Act of 1934–36. The overall impression gained from the reading of this case was that the judge was not so much citing precedents and laws as binding factors, but rather as *corroborative* materials to support his own assessment of the facts of the case. The case stands or falls primarily on the basis of the judge's evaluation of the reasonableness of the litigant's behavior and not by constraints imposed on his thinking by previous decisions.

The reasonableness of a judge is a key factor in his determination of the canons of reasonableness to be applied in other people's affairs. By this is meant not just the personality of the judge but also his legal philosophy, his social outlook, and the degree of formality in his thinking, as well as the cognitive process whereby he chooses one legal principle over another. Experienced lawyers have an uncanny sense for recognizing the reasonableness or unreasonableness of the judges before whom they submit their cases. They often base their presentations on this assumed personal knowledge to achieve a predicted favorable outcome. But the outcome is also a function of the random combination of judges at the different judicial levels. An example of one case, *Horton v. London Graving Dock Co. Ltd.* (1951), was tried at three separate judicial levels before a total of nine judges, the substantive issue being an accident that caused injury to a workman, and whether reasonable care had been taken under the circumstances. The single judge, at the first judicial instance, found for the defendants, but the Court of Appeal, comprised of three judges, reversed the decision and found for the plaintiff. The composition of five judges, at the subsequent appeal to the House of Lords, split into a majority opinion of three, reversing the Court of Appeal's decision, and a minority decision of two upholding it.

The plaintiff, Horton, was a subcontracted worker engaged in a fitting job in the hold of a ship. The staging on which he was working was defective, and although he complained about this inadequacy to the defendants' charge-hand shipwright, nothing was done to rectify it. Horton subsequently fell from the staging, sustaining injuries. His claim was, among other things, that the defendants had not taken reasonable care to make the premises safe. The arguments made at the various judicial instances appeared to have less to do with the matter of reasonable care than with the nature of the relationship between the plaintiff and the defendants. The arguments were focused on the mutual obligations obtaining between the parties, but these mutual obligations are a function of how the parties themselves are categorized by the judge. *Reasonable care* is defined as an obligation rather than as an independent concrete phenomenon. The plaintiff was categorized as an invitee and the defendants as invitors. Had the relationship been that of an employee vis-à-vis an employer, the outcome would have been different. Under these circumstances, however, since Horton was aware of the danger but continued to work despite this knowledge, the invitor of the work was under no further obligation toward the invitee regarding the dangerous state of the defective staging.

An observer, untrained in law, would probably have had to evaluate the situation solely on the basis of common sense. It is more than likely that he would have arrived at the simple conclusion that those responsible for having supplied the defective staging, and having been duely informed of the situation by the plaintiff, yet having done nothing to rectify it, were guilty of some degree of negligence. By this train of thought, the behavior of the defendants could be deemed to be unreasonable. It is quite possible that even the judges, as individuals, may have considered the behavior in question to be unreasonable, but that is not the point. As already mentioned, the legal issue was the nature of the relationship between classes of persons, the rights and obligations of these classes, and the classification of the defective staging itself as being either a "usual" or an "unusual" danger.

The rules, as established by precedent and applying in this case, are different from those applying to the relationship between an employer and an employee. Since there was no direct contractual relationship between Horton and the London Graving Dock Co. Limited, their respective statuses were those of invitee and invitor. The rules governing this relationship are less stringent than those applying to employee and employer. Much of the deliberations in this case centered on the fact that if the plaintiff was aware of the danger but continued to work, both the knowledge of the danger and his acquiescence freed the invitor from any further obligations. Again, this involves categorization. Was the worker *sciens* or *volens* or both[2]? Much argument also explored whether the danger was "usual," "unusual," or "unexpected." There are degrees of relativity involved here, since what might constitute unusual danger for an ordinary person might not be such for a professional who works every day under these conditions. The court of appeals had determined that the defective staging was an unusual danger for a welder working on a ship, and the fact that the welder knew about it did not transform it into a usual danger. Without going into all the technicalities necessitated by having to consider precedents, it is worthwhile to note the remarks of one of the dissenting judges, Lord Reid, at the hearing in the House of Lords.

> I do not deny that fixed rules have advantages: cases can be more readily decided, and people interested can perhaps forecast more accurately what the decision will be in any case. But in the realm of negligence, at least, rigid rules give rise to what I believe to be avoidable injustice. I see no reason to depart unnecessarily from the simple method of asking in any case what would a reasonable man in the shoes of the defendant have done. The test is subject to obvious limitations. In some cases it is impractical, and in many cases it is for one reason or another undesirable to make that which a reasonable man would do a legal obligation, but I see no such difficulty in this case. In this case I have no doubt that a reasonable man in the position of the appellants would have averted the danger which caused damage to the respondent by providing more adequate staging. Why then was it not the appellants' duty to do just this? I have come to the conclusion that to hold that there was such a duty would infringe no principle and would conflict with no binding or well-recognized authority.

In essence, these remarks of Lord Reid approximate the hypothetical conclusion of the nonlegally trained observer of the facts of the case. One can almost detect a sense of frustration behind Lord Reid's words. It is clear that modern judges are wary of using tests of reasonableness, when they have the alternative of applying rules that serve to maintain consistency and predictability—the logical demands of any system.

One domain in which standards of reasonableness have proven effective is that of maintenance to be paid in the event of marital separation or in instances where it is proven that the husband willfully neglected to maintain his family. The statutory directives are most clear in this respect, and the court receives a clear mandate to determine what is reasonable. Section 23(1) of the Matrimonial Causes Act of 1950 states:

> When a husband has been guilty of wilful neglect to provide reasonable maintenance for his wife and infant children of the marriage, the court, if it would have jurisdiction to entertain proceedings by the wife for judicial separation, may, on the application of the wife, order the husband to make such periodical payments as *may be just* [italics mine]; and the order may be enforced in the same manner as an order for alimony in proceedings for judicial separation.

A landmark case, establishing the yardstick of reasonableness in this context, is *Scott v. Scott* (1951), in which the judge states that "the word reasonable no doubt has to be interpreted against the background of the standard of life which he had previously maintained." The ensuing judicial process is no more than an arithmetical exercise, by means of which the husband's current income is calculated and weighed against the actual provision he had formerly made. This yardstick allows for maximum flexibility in determining what constitutes reasonable maintenance by virtue of its extreme simplicity. In *Roy-Lewis v. Roy-Lewis* (1954) the husband had deserted his wife, having formerly paid her £5 per week for housekeeping expenses. After the desertion, he reduced the weekly payment to £3, arguing that the wife could take up her former employment. The court, in arriving at its decision, also took into account the fact that the husband was now receiving an increased income from a trust settlement, which had boosted his net income from £480 in 1950 to £915 in 1954. Accordingly, the court awarded the wife an increased weekly payment of £6.

The arithmetical translation of reasonableness enables the courts to be less hesitant in matters of reasonable maintenance or reasonable income. Many judges feel so certain of the ground on which they stand in these cases as to describe their remedies as *objective* assessments. On the other hand, one might question this by raising the same element of uncertainty, applying to reasonableness in these specific contexts as would apply to its usage in other domains. A case pitting the element of uncertainty against reasonable income is *Re Golay's Will Trusts, Morris v. Bridgewater and Others* (1965). A will, drawn up by Golay, stated that "Mrs. B was to enjoy one of my flats during her lifetime and to receive a reasonable income from any other properties." The executor of the will considered that the specific clause relating to "reasonable income" was void because of its inherent uncertainty. The court rejected this position, agreeing that any subjective appraisal of what is reasonable would, of course, be inappropriate. But the judge said, quite categorically, that courts have had long experience in making *objective* assessments in such cases, so the matter could be brought to court for settlement, thus ruling out the voiding of the will on the grounds of uncertainty. The judge may well have been deluding himself in making the distinction between subjectivity and objectivity. There is no logical method whereby the concept of reasonableness may be objectively defined. The arithmetic, mentioned above, provides a comfortable illusion that reasonable maintenance is being provided. The semantic significance of the word *reasonable*, however, is that of uncertainty. Quite paradoxically, it is used throughout legal literature for its decisiveness. Cases are decided on the basis of the judge's assertion that "this is reasonable" or "that is unreasonable," the only *real* reason being that the judge has the authority to do so. While the courts may operate on the basis of agreed principles as to what might constitute reasonable maintenance or income, these principles are no more than wide parameters, within which the judge will ultimately be making his own subjective assessments. In *Davis v. Davis* (1966), some of the phrases employed by the judge clarify what underlies the arithmetic.

> If the wife has been accustomed during the marriage to live in a luxuriously appointed house, I think that she is entitled to ask for a lump sum payment of such an amount as will provide her with a

> standard of living commensurate with that to which she has been accustomed. I use the word "commensurate" advisedly, for I think it must be obvious that she can hardly expect exactly equivalent accommodation; it would not be "reasonable" to award enough for that. . . . Is the sum awarded by the judge then "reasonable" having regard to what the wife is entitled to expect? Such evidence as is before the court confirms, what I think must be common knowledge, that £15,000 does not go far towards purchasing house property in the sort of neighborhood where a woman with this background can reasonably expect to live.

Reasonable maintenance, then, is not just an objective exercise in arithmetic. The wife in *Le Roy-Lewis v. Le Roy-Lewis* can get by on £6 per week, whereas this would be considered as totally inadequate for the wife in *Davis v. Davis*. This falls far short of objectivity. Reasonable maintenance or reasonable income are not governed by an objective standard such as a calculation of a minimal standard of living as a base line, applicable to everybody regardless of social status[3]. In the absence of this, there has to be a subjective appraisal by the judge when he determines what is "commensurate" to the standard of living previously maintained by the wife. Once again, reasonableness is a qualifier of the judge rather than a qualifier of concrete reality.

This opens the argument over the relationship between law and politics, one of the more complex domains being that of administrative law. Earlier in this chapter, reference was made to Lord Greene's four parameters of motivation that the court would have to take into account when exercising its discretion to intervene or not. The remaining issue of "disregard of public policy" requires some clarification. Even though a distinction is drawn between "unreasonableness," and "disregard of public policy," the line between them is extremely thin, and it is here that the greatest likelihood of the politicization of law may occur. But that is perhaps less important than the overall issue of whether judges, who are called upon to assess administrative or executive actions, can arrive at value-free decisions. Just as many social scientists have serious reservations about "value-free" social science, the same doubts could be expressed about legal science. For in both instances, the two "sciences" are dealing with human actions. If this scepticism is correct, and judges are incapable of arriving at value-free decisions, then what values do they apply, and to what extent can these values be detached from their own personal social outlook or ideology?

Court decisions periodically evoke considerable public controversy. One such case, known as the Poplar Case, was *Roberts v. Hopwood* (1925). In 1920 the local borough of Poplar had a majority of elected socialist councilmen. Presumably in accordance with their ideological commitments, they decided to pay all council employees a minimum wage of £4 per week, this wage applying equally to male and female employees. Prior to this decision, the minimum wage had been £3-4-0 for men and £2-9-9 for women. The statutory authority for this decision was quite clear, the wording being that the council was entitled to "pay such salaries and wages as they *thought fit*" [italics mine]. The council's decision, however, was overruled by the court. Since courts are normally reluctant to intervene in matters of executive action, this particular court had to find convincing reasons for its decision. Following the council's decision in 1920, there had been a significant reduction in the cost of living throughout England, together with a correlated reduction in wages in the public sector. The court contended that augmented salaries went against the overall trend of the labor market at the time, and even if the council *saw fit* to pay these salaries, the court did not see it *as fit*. By virtue of its decision, the court decreed not only that the new rate of salaries was unreasonable, but that it was also illegal.

Had the argument been confined solely to the econometrics of the labor market, the decision could have been plainly understood as a straightforward economic calculation, quite impersonal and value-free in its motivation. But there are no straightforward economic calculations that can be said to have no political motivations or implications. The court did not conceal its value judgments when it used such terms as "eccentric principles of socialist philanthropy" or "feminist ambitions" in referring to the decision of the Poplar Council. The court might have claimed this was unreasonable administrative policy in light of prevailing economic conditions and left it at that, without the pejorative comments about the council's behavior. But given the terminology of the statute, the issue before the court, as always, was one of legality.

As has already been noted in an earlier case, reasonableness and legality are not synonymous. *Legality* has always been the convenient escape clause that has enabled the courts to avoid substantive issues. In this case, the statute could not have been clearer in its indication that the council was empowered to pay its employees as it sees fit. Furthermore, there was an additional element of vindictiveness, demonstrated by the court, in that it penalized the councillors by personally surcharging them for the discrepancy created by the payment of the augmented salaries. When the responsible ministry—the Ministry of Health—decided to waive the imposition of this demand on the councillors, the court went on to find the ministry's decision *ultra vires*.

The defenders of the Poplar decision claim that the councilmen had given disproportionate weight to improving the wages of the employees and, consequently, insufficient consideration to the taxpayers' interests. Such a rationalization has been made by Denning (1983:141). But this does not answer the terms of an even more basic question. On what grounds does the court choose to intervene in the substance of executive decisions, when its overall policy is not to intervene? Furthermore, can it be denied that the judge's remarks about "eccentric principles of socialist philanthropy" or "feminist ambition" are indicative of hostility? There can be no clear answers to these questions.

The reasonableness of administrative action is a problem that the presumptions of legal positivism are ill-equipped to handle. Honoré (1973:1) has accused sociologists of having entered the World Cup final between Positivists and Natural Lawyers, without learning the rules. He might have been more accurate had he said that sociologists, who might in fact have read the rules, did not accept them uncritically. One of the differences in approach between the lawyer, irrespective of his theoretical orientation, and the social scientist, is summed up in Hamnett's statement: "The specificity of the law then emerges as no more than the ideological charter of a particular professional group, and thus is subject to, rather than constitutive of, the anthropologist's analysis" (1977:4). In very blunt terms, this means that the spectators of the World Cup have as much to say about the game as the players and referees themselves, especially since the game is ultimately played for the benefit of the spectators.

The polemic is incidental only as a means to forestall criticism. It is apparent that natural justice, within recent years, has become more of a potent force in the sphere of administrative law, a point made by Schwartz and Wade (1972:320). Wade argues the case for natural justice even more strongly when he points out that there are both narrow and broad interpretations of the concept. Narrow interpretation places natural justice squarely within the existing rules of *ultra vires*, while the broader interpretation seems to be drawn from the American experience. In the absence of a constitution in England, Wade asserts, "Just as the broad constitutional guarantee of 'due process of law' has proved of such importance in the United States for the imposition of a general standard of justice, so in England the concept of natural justice should provide the legal foundation on which administrative procedure should rest" (1971:173). If natural justice has assumed any importance in the legal process, it is only as a function of the decisions of individual judges, who have departed from the normative timidity of the judiciary by placing executive actions under judicial review and, from time to time, overruling the outcomes of executive discretion. Judicial review is not in itself an expression of reasonableness but is a mechanism that enables the judge to apply his own criteria of reasonableness. It opens the way for a judge to consider the reasonableness of an action and to judge it in those terms. On the other hand, it does not mean that the judge will automatically arrive at a reasonable decision.

One of the foremost champions for judicial review in the recent history of the English legal system has been Lord Denning. Young has written that "it would probably be true to say that no judge since the war has had a greater influence upon the way in which administrative law has developed. The outstanding feature of that development has been the great extension of the scope of judicial review of administrative action" (1981:157). Denning's decisions are important not so much for the specific content of the individual decisions, but rather for their overall impact in challenging, or at least querying, some of the basic tenets of the philosophy of law. No judge has enjoyed the degrees of both adulation and outraged criticism as has Lord Denning. *Enjoy* seems to be the operative word, since one cannot be oblivious to Denning's massive ego, which emerges time and again from the lines of his autobiographical works. Denning appears to fit the role of Llewellyn's "grand style" judge. In *R. v. Sheffield Crown Court, ex parte Brownlow* (1980) Denning appears to accept Llewellyn's advocacy for "situation sense" by rejecting the formal approach of the narrow legal interpretation of the words of a statute. Instead he opts for the criterion of public policy, the justification being that this will bring about the "more sensible result."

There is, of course, a price to be paid for this approach. First, it reduces the element of certainty in the administration of law, which may prove highly inconvenient for the legal profession itself. Yet it must be remembered that the law does not exist solely for the benefit of its practitioners. The perhaps misguided, but nonetheless prevalent, view of the public is that the judiciary is a bastion of justice and the means for its dispensation, whatever that may mean. A second price to be paid is that when the judge overexercises his powers of review, it might be suggested that he is going against the original legislative intent of the statute, or even worse, supplanting the role of the legislature. This is not a catastrophe because if the judge interprets the legislative intent in such a way that the legislature finds it objectionable, the legislative body has the ultimate prerogative to subsequently alter the wording of the law. But a third price constitutes a more serious problem—the problem that is the crux of this book. If Denning advocates striving for the more sensible result in certain types of cases, such a result can only be the outcome of the judge's own personal and subjective outlook. *Sensible*, or, for that matter, *reasonable*, are value-laden words, and there is no way that the judge's own values will not filter through to the decision-making process as a consequence of this approach.

Where Lord Denning most clearly allows his biases to gain control over his legal thinking is in those cases involving some aspect of sexual morality. Denning is a man of deeply religious conviction and is obviously offended by sexual permissiveness. His position on abortion, for example, differs little from that of the extreme conservatives in the United States Supreme Court. In a speech at a House of Lords debate on a bill to amend the Abortion Acts, Denning argues, "It is not only Christian doctrine, but it is the doctrine of our law and our common law that the unborn child has a life of its own and a right of its own which is recognized by the law at least from the time of quickening" (Hansard. 6.12.1982). Christian doctrine may be relatively immutable in relation to changing secular law. Abortion laws create large arenas for public controversy, the courts being merely one such arena. On such a subject, judges are no less opinionated than any other member of the public. In the United States judges have been appointed to the Supreme Court on the basis of their generalized *opinions* on this issue. On several occasions Denning has used the forum of the court to express his personal opinions, in the strongest of terms, on matters of sexual mores. Much of this data has been collated by Geary (1981), and is briefly summed up here.

In a divorce case, *Bravery v. Bravery* (1954), Denning virtually assumes the role of a Barotse judge in the way he berates the errant husband. The latter had voluntarily undergone sterilization—described by Denning as "a shocking thing took place." What shocked Denning was the idea of sexual gratification without social responsibility, as well as the opportunities affording licentiousness. It might be argued that Denning gave vent to what he probably recognized as a minority opinion, precisely because his legal decision was the minority opinion on a panel of three judges. This gave him the opportunity to moralize excessively in his judgment. Denning does remain consistent on matters of sexual morality out of a deep sense of conviction.

In *Ward v. Bradford Corporation* (1972) the issue was one of a female student who had been expelled from a teachers' college for having had a man in her room in the residence hall after hours. There had been four other female students present at the time. Ward, having broken the rules, was expelled, but in a way that was procedurally questionable. Up to this time, the discretion to bring a student before the disciplinary committee had been the exclusive right of the principal. In the present case the principal had chosen not to bring the matter before the disciplinary committee. The board of governors, however, changed the rules, creating for itself the right to also submit cases before the disciplinary committee. This change in rules was applied *retroactively* in Ward's case—a clear example of a breach of natural justice, so championed by Denning. In this case Denning opted for a narrow reading of the rule that disallowed women from inviting men into the residence hall overnight, while totally ignoring the matter of the retroactivity. Again, Denning could not resist the role model of the Barotse judge, when he said, "This is a fine example to set others . . . and she is a girl training to be a teacher. . . . I expect the governors and the staff thought she was quite an unsuitable person for it. She would never make a teacher. No parent would knowingly entrust their child to her care."

An apt summation of Denning's brand of justice has been made by Schmitthoff.

> He looks at law as an instrument of doing justice . . . justice which is founded on what the majority of right thinking people regard as a fair solution, justice which the common people understand and which gives them confidence that those occupying the judgement seat do not live in a different world of ideas from their own and understand their hopes and anxieties. (1979:98)

In some cases Denning has faithfully fulfilled the role of a reasonable judge, in others he has not, but in all events he has raised questions about the philosophy of law that cannot be swept under the carpet.

Lord Denning is a self-proclaimed defender of the "stability and security of family life." In a speech given in the House of Lords on the subject of artificial insemination, Denning found the opportunity to fulminate against adulterers, homosexuals, and pornographers. The point is that if some of Denning's decisions are highly enlightened and others are seen as regressive, Denning is a reasonable or an unreasonable judge depending on the viewpoint of the observer. There is no way to escape this assessment, for both the grand and formal styles of judging will create injustices. Man-made systems are inevitably imperfect, particularly those that are human behavioral systems. The imperfections exist precisely for the reason that systems concerned with human behavior cannot be value-free. A legal system is no more value-free than any other social system, which means that the sciences that create these systems are also not value-free. This assertion, quite categorically, includes legal science.

The judge is in total control of the situation that obtains in the court and is the ultimate arbiter of what is reasonable or not. Even if some cases go before a jury, there is no guarantee that there will be a greater degree of reasonableness in the outcome than if the case had been heard by a judge or a panel of judges. The judge effectively controls the area of law finding in jury-tried cases and determines the parameters of the relevant facts. Juries and judges are supposed to reach their verdicts in the absence of "reasonable doubt"—perhaps one of the most cryptic phrases in legal terminology, leading to considerable confusion. What is the nature of the interaction between the judge and the jury in determining what might be considered reasonable doubt? In the case of *Stafford v. D.P.P.* (1974), new evidence was submitted after a jury conviction. Up until this time the judges had to reconsider a case in the light of how a jury *might* have addressed itself to the new evidence. From 1964 there was also an option to reorder a new trial by jury. But *Stafford v. D.P.P.* broke the rule by enabling the judges to appraise the new evidence themselves. Lord Devlin, in commenting on this case (1979:133), demonstrates some of the confusion in determining what is "reasonable doubt." The remarks of two of the three judges are supplied here.

> If the court has no reasonable doubt about the verdict, it follows that the court does not think that the jury could have had one; and, conversely, if the court says that the jury might, in the light of the new evidence, have a reasonable doubt, that means that the court has a reasonable doubt. (Viscount Dilhorne)
>
> It is, of course, true that two equally reasonable men may differ as to whether there is a reasonable doubt as to the guilt of the accused. But if I feel sure that he is guilty and you feel doubt on the point, I must regard your doubt on that point as unreasonable, however reasonable a person I consider you in general to be. Conversely, if I regard your doubt as reasonable, I cannot feel sure that the accused is guilty. (Lord Cross)

Devlin points out that only the ambiguity underlying the word *reasonable* allows for this interpretation of the judges, who are, in effect, saying here that the judges are the final arbiters of what is reasonable, and not the jury.

In another case, *Secretary of State v. Tameside Borough Council* (1976), Devlin quotes the judges' opinions on *reasonableness* in the general sense of its meaning,

> Two reasonable persons can perfectly reasonably come to opposite conclusions on the same set of facts without forfeiting their title to be regarded as reasonable. (Lord Salmon)
>
> History is replete with genuine accusations of unreasonableness when all that is involved is disagreement, perhaps, passionate, between reasonable people. (Lord Russell)

Devlin sums this all up as follows: An emotional, unreasoned decision is irrational; a wrongly reasoned decision is unreasonable. "The reasonable man, beloved of law, is a man who both uses his reason sensibly and arrives at a fair and moderate result" (1979: 134). At this point the confusion becomes immense. Is Devlin, when referring to the reasonable man, looking at the litigant's behavior or at the verdict of the judge and jury vis-à-vis that behavior or the opinion of the appellate judge on the given verdict?

There are different levels of reality involved here—the reasonableness of the substantive issue being judged and the reasonableness of the system that is doing the judging. On reexamining the range of legal cultures referred to in this text, one conclusion has to be that the legal culture of small-scale, noncomplex societies addresses itself to the reasonableness of the substantive issue in its attempt to supply a remedy. The subject matter of litigation, in broad categories, is not too different from what is to be found in our own society: criminal acts, torts, "contractual" relationships, as well as the whole range of personal law, marriage, divorce, and inheritance. The subject matter is not the important variable; what differentiates our legal culture from other legal cultures is the degree of systematization. Primitive legal cultures have little or no systematization, but the complexity of a modern legal system is such that the system itself makes demands on its practitioners far beyond the substantive issues with which it is involved. Hart's primary rules of obligation are sometimes obfuscated by the secondary rules of recognition, to the extent that the rules of recognition are transformed into primary rules, in the sense of their relative importance. The modern system is as much concerned with its own survival as it is with its function, which means, among other things, that a functional explanation of a legal system's *modus operandi* is simplistic and insufficient. By placing the modern system in a comparative and cross-cultural context, it is possible to see how the significance of the reasonable man, or simply reasonableness, has changed over time. The final chapter will look at those factors that might provide a better understanding for the changed attitudes toward reasonableness in the legal process.

Notes

1. The literal translation is "beyond powers." The term essentially means the excessive use of legal power or authority beyond what has been explicitly or implicitly conferred.
2. The terms *sciens* and *volens* refer to the state of mind of the individual at the time of the incident giving rise to litigation. *Sciens* implies that the individual had knowledge of the situation, and *volens*, in the cited context, refers to the principle *volenti non fit injuria*. This means that bodily harm suffered with the plaintiff's freely given assent is a defence in tort cases. The relationship with *sciens* is that knowledge is not in itself assent, but could be construed as evidence of assent.
3. As for example, such Social Security benefits as old-age pensions.

6

Conclusion

The transformation of the reasonable man into the reasonable judge is, conceptually, a cognitive process. Reasonableness is an evaluative perception of a situation. If in some legal cultures the standards of reasonableness are arrived at on the basis of a shared consensual understanding, this is not the case in a modern legal system where the sole arbiter of deciding what is reasonable is the judge himself. In comparing the legal culture of the Cheyenne with, say, the deliberations at the Queens Bench, the only basic common denominator is that a judgment is required in a situation wherein somebody had done something he should not have done, or refrained from doing something he should have done. The difference of perceptions, in either case, is a consequence of how the person's action, or inaction, is classified. Clearly, the Cheyenne perceive, classify, and order reality in a very different way from that of a judge in a modern court setting.

In both instances some act of contravention has occurred—among the Cheyenne or in the early stages of development of the kibbutz, it is a *shared understanding* that has been broken. In a complex society, such as our own, it is a *law* or a *rule* that has been infringed. The underlying social premise for this distinction is the presence or absence of an authority that is empowered to make laws and rules and, when necessary, be capable of enforcing compliance. If there is no such authority, Malinowski's notion of "mutuality" becomes a prime motivating force within the system of social control. But in those societies with defined authoritarian political structures, Radcliffe-Brown's adaptation of Pound's definition of law—"social control through the systematic application of force by the politically organized society"—constitutes the underlying social premise for modern legal thought, much as the profit-motivated "economic man" constitutes an axiom for formal economic thought. Both Malinowski and Radcliffe-Brown erred in assuming the exclusivity or universality of their definitions of law. At some points the definitions merge, for even in those societies with highly developed, centralized political systems, people may be obeying laws out of a recognition that, together with other persons, it is of mutual advantage and benefit to do so. Under these circumstances, this attitude might be the result of an inner compulsion and not merely a consequence of the fear of coercive sanctions. This has been suggested by some of the Scandinavian legal realists. By the same token, even in the most acephalous and anarchic society (such as the Eskimo of Greenland), outraged public opinion to a serious transgression can result in the most extreme sanction—death (Birket-Smith, 1924). However banal the contention, the key to the difference in legal thinking lies in the relationship between law and politics.

In those dispute situations where there is no authority capable of compelling an outcome, the alternative is to seek a remedy through negotiation or arbitration. The nature of reasoning is different in a process of adjudication from the reasoning required in arbitration and negotiation. In arbitration and negotiation only very diffuse and nonsanctioned coercive pressures can be brought to bear on a recalcitrant party to the dispute: supernatural sanctions, possible forfeiture of beneficial mutual relationships, and an adverse climate of public opinion. This element of public opinion is, perhaps, the most important pressure among those enumerated. Public opinion, in both its majority and minority expression, is a manifestation of the shared understandings held by the particular group.

The level of abstraction of a shared understanding is of a low order and is closely linked to the specifics of the case. Moreover, its expression tends to be sufficiently vague in order to create a significantly wide consensus for the idea itself. Llewellyn and Hoebel specifically noted that the Cheyenne were incapable of discussing their legal matters in detached and abstract terms. The underlying idea could not be clearly enunciated, and what remains is just a "feeling" about what is right or reasonable. The idea of reasonableness meets both these specifications, for not only is it case-oriented, but it is also extremely vague in its meaning. The concept of reasonableness exists, not by virtue of legislation but by the criteria whereby a culture socializes its members to recognize the principles governing life in that particular culture. Most people unquestionably accept these principles as reasonable, not only as a guideline for their own behavior, but also as a means to assess the behavior of others. These are not immutable principles. Hart was wrong in assuming that "primitive" law is fixed in time (1961:90). Changing conditions give rise to a constant reevaluation of existing principles, and their substitution by new principles is governed by both their relevance to, and reasonableness in the light of, the new conditions.

It has been pointed out that norms are not merely the external features of regular behavior patterns, observed and recorded by anthropologists and sociologists. A more realistic manifestation of norms is to be found in the situation where people have to publicly judge the behavior of others. In such conditions it is indeed possible that the norm may be stated as an ideally high standard of behavior. Alternatively, and especially in those societies where the judicial forum is incapable of imposing a solution, the norms are restated with appropriate leeways in order to effect a compromise or to persuade the disputing parties to accept the remedy. It is suggested here that a correlation exists between the way in which the norm is employed in the judicial process and the degree of power and authority vested in the judge.

Employing Fried's rough classification of political societies (1967), there is a greater likelihood of the use of norms, qualified by leeways, in the *egalitarian* societies, as exemplified in this text by the Kipsigis, Tiv, and kibbutz. Correspondingly, in the *ranked* societies, the Barotse being one such example, there will be a tendency toward reliance on a less flexible statement of the norm, a function of the difference between arbitration and adjudication. The former is a direct appeal to the reasonableness of the disputing parties and to public opinion, whereas the latter is more of a justification for the reasonableness of the judge's assessment of the facts of the case in arriving at a decision. The incipient transformation is a shift in emphasis from the whole-man approach in *gemeinschaft*-type societies to the consideration of the actions of the parties involved, without regard to the status of the individual disputant. The judge is looking at *classes* of individuals and *classes* of actions, which means that the substance of the case material is being considered at a higher level of abstraction. On this basis the judge has to rationalize the reasonableness of his decision. The norm begins to assume the role of a rule, and this is the point at which the reasonable man begins to give way to the reasonable judge.

The transition is clearly seen in the Kipsigis example. Prior to the establishment of national courts, the Kipsigis *kokwet* was virtually without power to impose a solution on a dispute. Even the traditional "jurisprudential" terminology of the Kipsigis[1]—*pitet*, meaning both "law" and "nature," and *sogorge*, meaning an "offender" as well as an "unnatural act"—is indicative of a mode of thought and is consistent with the lack of an authoritarian political structure. But it was also a useful basis for the determination of what is reasonable or not. "Natural" and "unnatural" share the same indeterminate characteristics as "reasonable." Furthermore, a case could not be resolved until both parties had formally given their assent to the proposed remedy. The case would be reheard time and again until the disputing parties were satisfied with the result. The very nature of the procedure was such that it was being directed toward an appeal to the reasonableness of the litigants. If it was unacceptable, the case remained unresolved. Different norms were cited at each hearing in order to persuade the litigants to accept a reasoned and reasonable solution. The change came about only when it became possible to bring cases before the local magistrate's court. This was essentially an appellate procedure in civil cases, since there was a stipulated prerequisite for a prior hearing at the *kokwet* level. The outcome was predictable. The statistical data indicate that the magistrate's court upheld most of the decisions taken at the *kokwet* level (see chap. 2). But now the decisions were enforcible. The old men of the *kokwet* soon realized that they no longer had to take such pains in appealing to the reasonableness of the litigants. Moreover, the increase in litigation among the Kipsigis, as a consequence of ever-growing involvement in a market economy, became progressively more time consuming within the traditional context. The wise old men, sitting under a tree, were fast becoming incipient bureaucrats. Decisions were made as a result of adjudication, and the former normative standards of reasonableness employed to justify the remedy had now become conveniently defined as "customary law." The indirect authority that had filtered down from the court to the *kokwet* is the most probable cause that would account for the transformation in the judicial logic.

Another case study in this text attempted to demonstrate how the ever-increasing centralization of power in a society has led to the bureaucratization of legal thought. The law is no longer concerned with the search for meanings in social relationships. The legislated formulas merely establish what these relationships ought to be. The comparative study of land law in medieval England and what is seen as analagous in Soga society illustrates this particular transformation. There is a subtle interaction between law, politics, and economics, the last assuming the role of a prime cause. The cash nexus between individuals depersonalizes the social relationship, and, correspondingly, the authority can depersonalize legal relationships by formulating them at higher levels of abstraction. The way centralized government achieved this was by recognizing the original sets of relationships, while at the same time transforming them from their original historical framework. Legal relationships were now restated as formulas at a much higher level of abstraction, which well served the bureaucratic interest. A system was beginning to emerge in which there was no place for subjective interpretations. But it was not just a matter of streamlining the legal system for its own sake. It was also a consequence of the conflict over power between the central authority and the diffuse loci of traditional powers at the periphery. The monarch in England and the African local government in Uganda were as much concerned with the consolidation of their powers as they were to provide universal standards for legal remedies. The provision of universal legal remedies and access to justice was merely one of the means employed by the central authority to weaken the power base of local rulers. The ultimate consequence of this process is that it is now the legislative body that determines the standards for behavior and the judiciary that interprets these standards.

Judges, unless faced with a particularly hard case, do not normally look for meanings underlying sets of social relationships. Their judgments are made on the basis of statements (i.e., laws, statutes, rules, and precedents) about these social relationships. If these statements impart any kind of meaning to social relationships, it is only in the highly abstracted sense of how behavior "ought to be." Under certain circumstances judges may be forced to consider the meaning of a law when they have to extrapolate what may have been its legislative intent. Most commonly, judges take a narrow view and limit themselves to the interpretation of the words contained in a statute. Such an approach leaves little room for the consideration of reasonableness as a judicial standard, unless the law specifically directs the judge to consider reasonableness as a relevant factor. In criminal law, the judge may only take "mitigating circumstances" into account when sentencing. In some of the other legal cultures discussed in this text, mitigating circumstances are precisely the grounds of reasonableness that the judge considers in order to arrive at a remedy.

The distinction between "verdict" and "remedy" is a real one. It reflects, in part, the Durkheimean dichotomy between repressive and restitutive law. It is true that not all modern law is repressive, unless Durkheim's intent is taken in the sense that all judicial decisions in a modern context are ultimately enforcible by coercive sanctions. The value of "ideal types" of this nature is only to be seen in the broadest of terms. Contrary to Durkheim's position, the main thrust of much of primitive law is to achieve some form of restitution, which is probably the reason why we do not find a distinction between civil and criminal law in many legal cultures. On the other hand, criminal law in modern society does little or nothing to compensate the victim of a crime. But what is important and relevant here is, given the overall difference between the aims of repressive and restitutive legal systems (verdicts as opposed to remedies), the thought processes of judges under either set of conditions are going to be different.

The modern judge, who is required to hand down a verdict and has the full backing of the state's coercive machinery to effectively do so by means of ensuring its compliance, is under no compulsion to appeal to the reasonableness of the parties, unless, of course, he is functioning in an arbitrative capacity. Furthermore, he is under the constraint of having to maintain standards of logical consistency in his application of the law. This does not enable him to examine the reasonableness of the situation before him on an *ad hoc* basis. In comparison, and in the absence of these aforementioned conditions, the judge in the nonmodern legal context has to rely heavily on the factor of reasonableness as a major part of his argumentation, given also that his primary aim is restitutive. If the modern judge is ideally required to be a logician, his primitive counterpart is a pragmatist par excellence.

In modern society the true arbiters of reasonableness are to be found in the legislative branch of the political system. It is here that the rules for behavior are drafted and enacted. The judges can, to a lesser degree, also "make law" by interpreting existing law, by judicial review, by judicial discretion, and by the finding of gaps within the existing law. But as a general matter of principle, the judiciary is the subordinate element within the overall political system. Even if in theory the judiciary has the autonomy to review the reasonableness of an executive action, it more often than not, can conveniently escape this task by confining itself exclusively to the legal validity of that action. Validity, in this sense, rests on factors beyond the intrinsic reasonableness or unreasonableness of the action itself. It is usually argued that this is precisely the task of the judiciary—to consider the legality of an action, and only that. But one of the consequences of this attitude is that the rule of law, as an ideology, may well be sacrificed to the rules of the game.

The literature of the sociology of law is replete with accusations against the judiciary, a common theme being that the judiciary has a vested interest in supporting the establishment, especially in a conservative establishment. Generally, this is an accurate assessment, but the criticism of this principle should be put in proper perspective. It is incontestable that one of the tasks of the judiciary is to maintain law and order as determined by the legitimate authority. But it can also be argued that there are limits to this position. It was certainly an insufficient defense for the judges of the Third Reich in Germany. In the normal context of a liberal democracy, however, difficulties arise when issues of public policy have to be deemed as reasonable, or not, by the judiciary.

The occasional landmark case poses the nature of the dilemma before the judge. In *Liversidge v. Anderson* the majority considered that the secretary of state was under no obligation to disclose his reasons for Liversidge's detainment order, given the conditions of war at that time. By evading the examination of the substantive issues underlying the secretary's decision, the court was essentially saying that it was satisfied that the secretary's action was legal. Had they left the matter at that, the logic of the decision could be plainly understood. But by referring to the wartime conditions, they had introduced a substantive element into the argument, which was implicitly also arguing for the reasonableness of that decision. The dissenting minority opinion was also a value judgment, influenced by a natural justice concept of an individual's right to liberty. It demanded that the secretary's reasons be disclosed so that it could be determined whether or not he had "reasonable cause." If, presumably, the secretary could not demonstrate that he had reasonable cause, then his action could be deemed illegal, precisely because it was unreasonable. It matters little that most of the argumentation in this case revolved around the meaning of the words describing the secretary's authority. The court was simply fulfilling its obligations to the rules of the game, but it is certainly a matter of opinion as to whether the rule of law was being upheld. The matter of opinion is largely a function of the ideological outlook of the judge himself. To complicate the issue even further, the matter of opinion is also that of the observer, who comments on the decision of the judge. A two-tiered phenomenon is involved here—the reasonableness of the act that is being judged and the reasonableness of the judge in the making of his decision—and a distinction between the two must be made.

It is at this juncture that the question arises whether judges, when conforming to professional rules, do indeed have complete autonomy in arriving at decisions. The unfortunately obtuse answer is that although the possibility of total autonomy exists for the supposedly *separate* branch of government, judges, nonetheless, voluntarily restrict themselves from employing their full political potential. In other words, the judiciary subordinates itself to the executive branch of government.

An example illustrating the ambivalence of judges toward matters of public policy is taken from the proceedings of the Israeli High Court of Justice (to be distinguished from the Israeli High Court of Appeals, although the same justices sit in either capacity)[2]. The High Court of Justice, among other things, deliberates on pleas for relief against executive actions. Many arguments based on concepts of natural justice are heard in this court. The history of this court reveals an inconsistent employment of judicial review, using a technique that governs access to the court through requirements of standing. These requirements are raised and lowered in accordance with the court's periodic involvement in sensitive political issues. The emergent pattern is that soon after the court has handed down a number of controversial decisions on "sensitive issues," it has raised the standing requirements, and a period of noninvolvement follows.

Shapiro (Jerusalem Post, 21 January 1987) has pointed out that until 1970 "it was accepted practice not to raise issues of standing in cases involving matters of fundamental rights." But in 1968 the court handed down a landmark decision concerning the registration of children of mixed marriages as Jews in *Shalit v. Ministry of Interior* (1968). Shortly afterwards the court also issued an order against the government, upholding the operation of the television authority on Friday nights (Orthodox Jewish rules of the sabbath had, up to this time, prevented television broadcasts on Friday nights). Both of these decisions went against the government's interest in maintaining coalition agreements with religious political parties. Two subsequent cases on sensitive religious issues—*Becker v. Ministry of Defence* (1970) and *Meron v. Ministry of Labour* (1970)—were dismissed by the court on the grounds of standing requirements, even though the government defendants had not themselves raised the issue of standing requirements. Shapiro goes on to quote one of the justices involved, Justice Witkon, who said,

> To the extent that the complaint has more of a public character and relates to matters that buzz in the political arena and serve as a subject for deliberations before the government and the Knesset, it is necessary to be more stringent with regard to standing requirements . . . otherwise there would be a violation of the principle of the separation of powers between the coordinate branches, with the court becoming something of a mini-parliament.

This last sentence appears to highlight the paradoxical elements in the concept of the separation of powers. The judge is addressing himself to the coordinate branches of government. If they are indeed coordinate, this could be interpretated to mean that a degree of equality is accorded to each branch. Even if the legislature is *primus inter pares*, if not dominant in its sovereign status, the relationship between the judicial and executive branches constitutes the problematic relationship. The judge just cited correctly asserts that it is not the function of a court to become a miniparliament. This is a highly convenient escape clause, since the matter that had been brought before the court concerned the actions of the executive branch, to be measured and assessed against existing legislation. In plain language, one of the implications of the idea of "coordinate branches" is that the judiciary has the right to review the legal validity of executive action. It is not clear from the judge's statement about the separation of powers whether he is speaking of a matter of principle or whether he is overconcerned with the court's image in the public eye. If judges are prepared to examine the reasonableness of situations in torts, personal law cases such as marriage and divorce, traffic offenses, and certain types of contractual relationships, why the reluctance to considering the reasonableness of executive actions? Some clues may be found in the deliberations of some structuralist sociologists, who have addressed themselves to the overall working of the system.

Luhmann only accords a degree of autonomy to the legal branch. For him, society is integrated not in terms of Durkheimean normative consensus, but rather in the framework of what he calls "compartmentalization." By dividing the social order into compartmentalized social subsystems, conflicts can be confined to within the subsystems themselves. Luhmann defines this process of integration as the "avoidance of a situation in which the operation of one subsystem produces unsolvable problems in another system" (1977:242). On face value, this last statement would appear to describe the reluctance on the part of the judiciary to deal with the reasonableness of executive action. The strategies employed to achieve this avoidance are termed by Luhmann "the reduction of complexities." His argument involves making a distinction between what he delineates as the *normative* and *cognitive* approaches to reality: the normative is inflexible and does little to reduce complexities, whereas the cognitive approach to expectations can make pragmatic readjustments to reality and thus alter expectations. Where the normative stands in stark contrast to the cognitive is the claim, usually on moral grounds, that even if the expectation is not realized, the norm itself nonetheless remains valid.

But Luhmann argues that the validity of law is not to be found in the premises of an objective order of principles of natural law, based on morality, justice, or ethics. He claims that "Positive law is made valid by decisions; a law of any content whatsoever can gain legitimate legal validity; and the same decision that makes a law a valid one can also withdraw its validity. . . . it is the very alterability of law that is the foundation for its stability and its validity" (1982:94). Even if this position is absolutely clear for its functionalist-positivist logic, it has been demonstrated as untenable in a recent paper[3] (Saltman and Rosenfeld, 1990). Our objection in that paper was that Luhmann's functionalist-positivist theory lacks any realistic evaluation of the decisions and actions within the system, and we concurred with Habermas, who has written,

> The unobjectionable manner in which a norm comes into being, that is, *the legal form of a procedure* guarantees as such only that the authorities which the political system provides for, and which are furnished with certain competencies and recognized as competent within that system, bear the responsibility for valid law. But the authorities are part of a system of authority which must be legitimized as a whole if pure legality is able to count *as an indication* of legitimacy. In a fascist regime, for example, the legal form of administrative acts can have at best a masking function. (1975:100, italics mine)

We stated in that same paper that Luhmann's main failure is his nonrecognition of the high-handed manner in which modern states perform on a day-by-day basis. We find that the active results of law tend to follow the direction taken by the dominant political forces. In the present context it is argued that if judges adopt a pragmatic stand for reducing complexities by avoiding the substantive issues, it is questionable whether they are fulfilling their responsibilities. The last sentence in the quotation from Habermas should be seen as a *caveat*, no less than a correct observation.

Althusser's idea of the "relative autonomy" of systems (1970:17–27) does not provide a satisfactory explanation either for the specific query raised here. Thompson's bitter critique of Althusser on the subject of law is well taken.

> Relative autonomy, on the contrary, has been lovingly elaborated, over many pages, and reappears as "instances," "levels," "differential temporalities," "dislocations" and "torsions." . . . . But how might we put such a concept to work? Is law, for example, relatively autonomous, and, if so, autonomous of what, and how relatively? . . . For I found that law did not keep politely to a level but was at every *bloody* level; it was imbricated within the mode of production and productive relations themselves (as property rights, definitions of agrarian practice) and it was simultaneously present in the philosophy of Locke; it intruded brusquely within alien categories, reappeared bewigged and gowned in the guise of ideology; it danced a cotillion with religion, moralising over the theatre of Tyburn; it was an arm of politics and politics was one of its arms; it was an academic discipline subjected to the rigours of its own autonomous logic; it contributed to the definition of the self-identity both of rulers and of ruled; above all it afforded an arena for class struggle within which alternative notions of law were fought out. . . . I am also arguing that Althusser's constructions are actively *wrong* and thoroughly misleading. His notion of 'levels' motoring around history at different speeds and on different schedules is an academic fiction. For all these 'instances' and 'levels' are in fact human activities, institutions and ideas. We are talking about men and women in their material life, in their determinate relationships, in their experience of these, and in their self-consciousness of this experience. (1978:96–97)

Polemics should not be dismissed merely because there might be a pejorative connotation to the very idea of the use of polemics in academia. An angry academic, angry over a social issue, is no more subjective than his supposedly detached colleague who deals with the same issue. The purity of objectivity in social science is dubious. There is much truth in what Thompson has to say here. Legislation and judicial decisions fall into all the categories that he enumerates. Judges cannot escape the fact that by either addressing an issue or avoiding it, they are still making an ideological statement.

Laws and judgments are utterances, not just geared to the structuralists' systemic requirements for a form of social control, but are also statements about the *specific* nature of a *particular* form of social control. From the standpoint of a linguist, Vološinov claims that "the immediate social situation and the broader social milieu wholly determine—and determine from within, so to speak—the structure of an utterance" (1985:53). In trying to understand his statement with reference to legal language, the "immediate social situation" is seen as the forum wherein laws are created, and the other forum where the laws are applied. The "broader social milieu" of these two arenas is nothing more than the ideological statements of how things *ought* to be, drafted and restated in accordance with professional specifications. Laws enacted in Parliament and verdicts handed down in courts are formulated in a milieu far removed from what Thompson has described as "men and women in their material life, in their determinate relationships, in their experience of these, and in their self-consciousness of this experience." The element of determination *from within* seems to play a relatively limited role. The Man on the Clapham Omnibus is more of a condescending joke than a legal reality.

Most judges willingly conform to the constraints laid upon them. They are part of the establishment, and it is not unreasonable that they should be supportive of the establishment to which they belong. The establishment, in determining the rights and duties of the citizenry through its political institutions, in no small way represents vested interests in the society. Judges are expected to uphold the system, irrespective of its ideological orientation. In this respect there are no biased judges, since their professional commitment should transcend their own ideological beliefs. The maintenance of the system is a far more important consideration than the substantive content of, say, executive action. For this reason judges are mostly reluctant to consider the reasonableness of such actions. If, on comparately rare occasions, some judges go against this trend, it can still only be achieved within given professional parameters.

Bell (1983:10–21) has described three models for judicial intervention in policy decisions. All three models supply criteria by which the judge is enabled to apply standards of reasonableness. The consensus model takes into account the difference between the thinking of the legislator, who enacts a law, and that of the judge, who by his decision may be "making" a law. The legislator, exercising his own personal opinions, only has to take the consensus into account as a possible factor that might influence his potential for remaining in power. The judge, bound by impartiality and professional commitment, can do little more than "keep the legal standards in step with current consensus" (ibid., 12). Consensus, however, is viewed narrowly in this context. It is not the judge's intuitive evaluation of public opinion. Bell is, in fact, referring to fundamental values that are already embodied in the laws and institutions of society. This enables the judge, in Bell's words, to legislate "within the framework of existing legal principles and rules, by *developing* principles rather than *creating* new ones" (ibid., 13, italics mine). Under these obligatory circumstances of having to examine fundamental values, there is no way in which he can avoid the consideration of the relative reasonableness of these values. It must be emphasized, however, that this does not necessarily require the judge to look at the reasonableness or, correspondingly, the lack of reasonableness in the actions of the parties concerned. The terms of reference are primarily the reasonableness of the abstract *statements* made about peoples's behavior, namely the rules, laws, precedents, and so on. The judge enters the realm of open-ended standards, which requires great skill on his part in finding his way through this sort of legal minefield. The unskilled judge may indeed be sorely tempted to employ his own intuitive evaluation of the consensus of public opinion, or what he may consider to be the majority opinion, or even worse, what he himself may consider to be reasonable.

The second model is Dworkin's theory of rights (ibid., 87–92). There is an implicit value judgement in Dworkin's theory, which can serve as a basis for the assessment of reasonableness. Assuming that the rights of individuals take precedence over the collective welfare, it is up to the judge to determine whether the individual's claim to a right is correct or not. As noted in the discussion on the Scandinavian legal realists, "rights" have no concrete standing in reality, beyond the fact that they have been declared as such, and that people actually believe they possess them. Dworkin's ideal judge goes beyond looking at the words of a statute (which may provide no remedy for the settlement of hard cases) and looks instead at the institution itself—its aims, functions, and purposes—all this in order to determine the nature of rights. He dismisses the vague background rights that may derive from considerations of justice, morality, or ethics. By looking at rights in the substantive context of an institution's activities, the judge has to make assessments based on reasonableness. Once having established the nature of the right, he can pit it against his evaluation of the collective welfare and arrive at a decision. Bell takes Dworkin to task for overstepping the judicial boundary, thus entering the legislative domain and making decisions that concern the collective welfare. In response to this criticism, it has been argued throughout this book that this is precisely where the autonomy of the judiciary should lie. Dworkin is not arguing for random interference in the affairs of the other branches of government. The determination of an individual's rights, as specified by Dworkin, is the product of a reasoned intellectual exercise. Moreover, if most judges are consciously or unconsciously assuming a conservative position through their narrow interpretation of the written law, there is no less justification for Dworkin's ideal, and activist judge to adopt a liberal stance by supporting the individual's rights, when there is justification for doing this.

The third model, which Bell calls the "interstitial legislator model," accords the judge the greatest degree of freedom in exercising his own judgment. It is, however, only relevant when there is no definitive legal solution to a problem. This is Hart's "grey area," or the "indeterminacy" noted by Stone. According to Bell, the judge in this situation chooses the option he considers to be the most beneficial to society at large. The judge has to put himself in the position of the legislator. This means that his thought processes are not strictly judicial, but essentially approximate those of the legislator. It is an expression of a personal ideological opinion. For Bell this is acceptable, if not in principle, at least in practice, since he writes it off as "making good minor deficiencies in the existing legal framework" (ibid., 19).

Bearing in mind that the major topic is that of reasonableness and not public policy per se, the relative virtues of these three models are not a question for evaluation here. Suffice that all three models allow for a broader interpretation of law, greater autonomy to the judiciary, and the opportunity for the judge to employ the criterion of reasonableness in his decision making. The last factor ought to mean that the judge is obligated to look at the facts of the case in order to assess the substantive issues, as opposed to merely interpreting the words of a statute. It is, however, recognized that even if judges were to employ their skill in their determination of what constitutes reasonableness, there is no guarantee that the outcome would necessarily be reasonable.

As noted, the interstitial legislator model accords the judge the same privileges as the legislator. Under such circumstances the judge would be making a value judgment about the best possible option *he* would consider as the most beneficial to society. This would clearly be a function of the judge's personality, ideology, and general world outlook. The consensus model is not too different, because if the judge has to assess the "fundamental values that are already embodied in the laws and institutions of society," the options are still open to him to apply his own personal interpretations regarding what these fundamentals might be. Lord Denning, for example, had explicit views on sexual mores, which undoubtedly indicated the fundamental values that influenced his decision making. On the other hand, some of the most reasonable decisions in the history of law have been made as a consequence of this approach. Only Dworkin's approach implies a specific direction. For those who value individual liberties, Dworkin's theory of rights would seem eminently reasonable.

The remaining question is, who are the judges? What political factors and social outlooks could possibly influence judges' perception of reasonableness? Some differentiation has to be made when relating to the senior judiciary, on the one hand, and their lower-ranking counterparts (particularly lay justices and stipendiary magistrates), on the other. The importance of the magistrates should not be underestimated, since the vast bulk of cases are tried by them and mostly go by unscrutinized and unreported. As trial judges they are engaged primarily in fact finding, and their evaluation of the facts is routine, decisive, and given to scrutiny only on appeal or as a result of a diligent journalist's critical investigative reporting. In the United States, local-level judges are elected by the community. The candidates publicize their views and political ideologies as part of an open election campaign. This process of electing judges is an overt political act. At another level, presidential nominees for Supreme Court appointments are subjected to open congressional hearings, during which the nominee's political and social points of view are closely examined. The composition of the Supreme Court is recognized as a conservative or a liberal one, and either composition is a function of political pressure successfully applied by the president.

The appointment of justices in Britain is a less strident affair than in the United States, it being a nonpublic issue. But the source of all appointments is political, be it the Lord Chancellor (himself a cabinet minister), who together with an advisory committee appoints justices, or the cabinet's recommendation to the Crown for the appointment of superior judges. In a letter sent to the advisory committees (as reported in the *Times*, 3 December 1966), the Lord Chancellor sets out the *ideal* guidelines for the appointment of justices: "The Lord Chancellor cannot disregard political affiliations in making appointments, not because the politics of an individual are a qualification or a disqualification for appointment, but because it is important that justices should be drawn from all sections of the community and should represent all shades of opinion."

Despite the doctrine, the reality is that the British judiciary at all levels is drawn preponderantly from the upper echelons of the society's class structure. Griffith provides a statistical breakdown of judges by social class origins, which lends credence to this assertion. For some, this does not constitute a problem. Jackson, commenting on the Lord Chancellor's directive, makes an amazingly patronizing statement: "Benches do tend to be middle to upper class, but that is a characteristic of those set in authority over us, whether in Town Hall, Whitehall, hospitals and all manner of institutions. I think that ordinary people are much more concerned with courtesy and efficiency than with these considerations of social class" (1967:183). It is well-nigh impossible to prove that decisions taken by the judiciary are influenced by the judges' class associations. Undoubtedly there are decisions of this nature, but the mechanical relationship between the decisions and the class associations of the decision makers is not demonstrable. Even an attempt to read the autobiographies or collected essays of retired judges, which often give vent to their personal opinions, yields no clear trend to the existence of such a relationship.

Many of the conclusions here, however, concur with those of

Griffith, but for different reasons. By placing modern legal thought in a cross-cultural (and thus comparative) context, the flaws and imperfections of the modern system are highlighted. The "primitive" judge enjoys a number of advantages over his modern counterpart, particularly as regards the degrees of freedom within which he operates. The nature of simple, small-scale societies is such that the homogeneity gives rise to a clear recognition of shared understandings both by the judges and those who are judged. These shared understandings also form basic guidelines that are essential for the everyday functioning of the society. People abide by these shared understandings, again, out of an awareness that it is beneficial to do so. This should not imply an idyllic portrait of a Rousseau's noble savagery. There are conflicts, deviations, and litigation in these societies, but there is also a calculated awareness of the importance of maintaining mutuality. If the Scandinavian legal realists speak of an inner compulsion to obey rules, it is not because of people's inherent nobility. It is rather the product of a pragmatic consideration that it is to the individual's advantage to maintain reasonably good relationships with the other members of this society. This has also been discussed by Shenker in his analysis of intentional communities.

In such societies the deviance of an individual evokes an emotional response from others on a scale ranging from extreme outrage to a relatively calm appraisal of that person's reasonableness, or lack of it. It is the deviant himself, and his relationship to others, that are the constituents of the problem, more than the specific deviant act. In small-scale societies everybody is known, to a greater or lesser degree, to everyone else. This makes it feasible to make judgments *ad hominem*, in total disregard of logical consistency. The aim of the judicial process is directed more toward remedying the effects of the specific problem and restoring the *status quo ante* than in punishing the offender, although such punishment is not precluded as a means for effecting a settlement. In many noncomplex societies there is no intermediate legislative agency that formulates predetermined and authoritative statements about normative behavior. Given the highly personalized nature of the situation and the absence of an independent authority, the "primitive" judge is not constrained by considerations of either the directives of the authority or by the need to maintain high standards of logical consistency in his decision making. The judge's appraisal of the common good is his own perception of the prevailing public consensus. Since, in most cases, he does not occupy an exclusively specialized role as a judge but has additional roles similar to those of all the other members of the society, he is in an excellent position to be fully aware of the consensus. He shares the same daily experiences with the litigants who stand before him. He does not have to search for fundamental principles in the existing law or rely on the interstitial legislator's model in order to reach a decision. If used skillfully, the common language of reasonableness becomes an effective tool for achieving a remedy. If, on the other hand, his appraisal of the consensus is flawed or his outlook biassed, his opinions will no longer be respected over time, and both his influence and effectiveness will be diminished. This stands in contrast with the professional and "authorized" judge, whose decisions are accepted as valid, not for their intrinsic reasonableness but by virtue of their authoritative source.

In the broadest of terms, the differences between judging in noncomplex and complex societies are both quantitative and qualitative. Before going on to clarify this, it must be pointed out that there are also some very basic similarities. Many issues requiring judgment, which face both types of society, are identical. This holds true even if there might be differing cultural perceptions about the meanings of these issues—a theft is a theft anywhere. By the same token, the broad categories of breaches of contract, negligence leading to damage, property rights, and the personal law of marriage, divorce, and inheritance are universal phenomena. Specific cases in these domains can be as complicated in simple societies as in contemporary modern society. The quantitative difference is the relative range of relationships that exist both in reality and potentially. In complex society this range is vast. The quantitative is not to be divorced from the qualitative, for the demographic differences between simple and complex societies give rise to a characteristically impersonal set of relationships between individuals in modern society. This in turn influences the degree of detachment of those called upon to judge these relationships. In such a situation, *ad hoc* standards of reasonableness, applied *ad hominem*, are no longer effective tools for achieving remedies. Mutuality is a weak cohesive factor in large-scale societies. The standards are now legislated and systematized at a high level of abstraction. The legislators may well believe that their enactments are reasonable, for they perceive them in terms of the overall welfare of the community at large. But these are the perceptions of only those authorized to create these standards, and the consensus around them is not solid.

The system, once established, has a life of its own. A great deal of human activity is directed toward the preservation and maintenance of the system, above and beyond the fulfillment of the needs of the individual, which the system purports to satisfy. Nonetheless, there exists the widespread belief that systems are ultimately instrumental in the satisfaction of individual needs. The fulfillment of the systems' demands is perhaps no less important than the actual services provided by these systems. For systems not only order human behavior for the intellectual convenience of their practitioners, they also stipulate the rules of the game, the rational guidelines on which people actually model their behavior. Rational economic behavior, for example, can be performed only in accordance with the guidelines of a given economic system. Similarly, people do things or refrain from doing things on the basis of the rationalization that "this is the law" or "this is against the law."

The substantive content of systems is little more than an ideal expression of expected and predicted behavior. If and when systems change to accommodate to the reality of changing normative patterns of behavior, it is at a slower pace. If judges have a conservative tendency, this is as much a consequence of the conservatism of the legal system itself as it is an implication of the judges belonging to a politically conservative social class. The law, in its constant striving to maintain logical consistency and achieve a high standard of predictability, does not keep pace with ongoing changes in social mores. A reasonable judge is one who understands the importance of timing in making a radical decision. He also recognizes that he is locked into a political system, within which he occupies a subordinate role. The overextension of judicial review and the use of judicial discretion can boomerang, given that the other branches of government have the potential to override the judge's decision by introducing the appropriate legislation. An unreasonable judge, however, is one who is ideologically committed to conservatism.

The demise of the reasonable man is not necessarily the death of all that is reasonable in the law. It is a transformation from an original state in which the judiciary looked at and examined social relationships in terms of their social and cultural meanings. The interpretation of these meanings derived from the shared understandings of the community regarding how things "ought to be." It was this type of understanding that accorded validity to judicial decisions of this nature. If, as previously indicated, legal validity is no more than a belief that a law is valid, judicial emphasis given to meanings plays a more powerful role in bolstering that belief. It is certainly a more convincing validation than the mere citation of the system's innate logic. The process of transformation involved a conscious logical exercise in the classification of persons, objects, and actions and the authoritative declaration of the principles underlying the relationships between these categories. Among other things, these principles were shaped by the system's requirement for consistency. Today's reasonable man, or more simply, *reasonableness*, is a concept circumscribed by legal logic and political considerations. It is an authoritative statement that is valid only because it has been made by the appropriate authority and because people believe it to be valid. It is a cognitive issue and has no place in the realm of concrete facts. As Lord Atkin put it so aptly in his minority decision in *Liversidge v. Anderson*, there is a difference between the ideas that the secretary of state "has reasonable cause" and the secretary of state "thinks he has reasonable cause." While the former is an authoritative statement, the latter is no more than a description of a person's state of consciousness. These are very different ideas. In comparing the majority and minority decisions in this case, reasonableness becomes merely a reflection of the attitudes of the person making a decision.

Three judges, well-versed in the rationale of their discipline, are incapable of arriving at a consensus in their interpretation of a legal statement. *Interpretation* is the operative word here, since the judges are engaged in a hermeneutical exercise rather than conforming to the more rigorous standards of explanation demanded by a science. For essentially, there is nothing to be explained by the law. Moreover, there are really no means whereby their respective conclusions can be validated or falsified beyond the process of a majority or minority decision. If judging is based, in part, on the *interpretation* of texts, the claim for a legal science is weakened. But even if, for the sake of argument, one allows the claim to legal science, there is still a discrepancy between the rationale of that claim and the activities of legal practitioners. It is the latter that bolsters the suspicion that there may be a certain "emperor's clothes" quality about many aspects of the law.

For all these reasons, reasonableness by virtue of its indeterminacy is antithetical to the ideally logical demands made by advocates for a legal science. The notion of reasonableness, however, may yet return to play an important role in the overall sphere of legal remedies. The overloading of courts by time-consuming, complex litigation, as well as the ever-increasing costs of such litigation, serves to encourage people to seek alternative solutions by such means as arbitration. It is in a process of this nature that reasonableness becomes an effective tool.

Notes

1. The dual meaning of the word *pitet* can only be understood in the context of the sentence in which it is used. An example of the word *sogorge* was given by an informant as "a cow that eats meat." The consistency in the use of these concepts, indicating the relationship between law and nature, is clear. A third idea is that of *chupge*—the literal meaning being "the bringing of a curse upon oneself"—and is the outcome of the performance of an offence, perceived as an unnatural act bringing into play a supernatural reaction.
2. The Israeli Supreme Court functions in a number of capacities. It is the highest appellate court dealing with both criminal and civil cases. In its capacity as a High Court of Justice, it becomes a court of first instance for the purpose of granting relief in the interests of justice.
3. The paper addresses itself to the incident known as the 300 Bus Incident, which took place in Israel in April 1984, in which two apprehended Arab hijackers of the bus were subsequently killed by the general security service. This was followed by an attempted government cover-up of the whole affair. The paper examines the reaction of the legal system to the events.

References

Allot, A. 1980. *The Limits of Law*. London: Butterworths.

Althusser, L. 1970. *Reading Capital*. New York: Pantheon.

Aubert, V. 1983. *In Search of Law*. Oxford: Martin Robertson.

Barnes, B., and D. Bloor. 1982. "Relativism, Rationalism and the Sociology of Knowledge." In *Rationality and Relativism*, ed. Hollis, M. and S. Lukes. Oxford: Blackwell.

Bell, J. 1983. *Policy Arguments in Judicial Decisions*. Oxford: Clarendon Press.

Ben-Rafael, E. 1979. "Dynamics of Social Stratification in Kibbutzim." *International Journal of Comparative Sociology* 21(1–2):88–100.

Birket-Smith, K. 1924. "The Country of Eggedesminde and Its Inhabitants." *Medelelser om Gronland* Copenhagen.

Bohannan, P. 1957. *Justice and Judgment among the Tiv*. London: Oxford University Press.

______ 1965. "The Differing Realms of Law." *American Anthropologist* 67, pt. 2.

Cairns, H. 1959. "The Community as the Legal Order." In *Community*, ed. Carl, J. Nomos II. New York: Liberal Arts Press.

Cardozo, B. 1921. *The Nature of the Judicial Process*. New Haven: Yale University Press.

Chanock, M. 1985. *Law, Custom and Social Order: The Colonial Experience in Malawi and Zambia*. African Studies ser. 45. Cambridge: Cambridge University Press.

Cotran, E. 1963. *Report on Customary Criminal Offenses in Kenya*. Nairobi: Government Printer.

Denning, A. 1983. *The Closing Chapter*. London: Butterworths.

Devlin, P. 1979. *The Judge*. London: Oxford University Press.
Diamond, A. S. 1956. Review of *The Judicial Process among the Barotse of Northern Rhodesia* by M. Gluckman. *International and Comparative Law Quarterly* 5:627–28.
Dworkin, R. 1975. "Hard Cases." *Harvard Law Review* 88(6).
______ 1977. "Is Law a System of Rules?" In *The Philosophy of Law*, ed. Dworkin, R. London: Oxford University Press.
Erasmus, C. 1977. *In Search of the Common Good*. New York: Free Press.
Fallers, L. 1956. *Bantu Bureaucracy*. Chicago: Chicago University Press.
______ 1969. *Law Without Precedent*. Chicago: Chicago University Press.
Frank, J. 1949. *Courts on Trial: Myth and Reality in American Justice*. Princeton, N.J.: Princeton University Press.
Fried, M. 1967. *The Evolution of Political Society: An Essay in Political Anthropology*. New York: Random House.
Geary, R. 1981. "Lord Denning on Sexual Morality." In *Justice, Lord Denning and the Constitution*, ed. Robson, P., and P. Watchman. Westmead: Gower.
Gluckman, M. 1955. *The Judicial Process among the Barotse of Northern Rhodesia*. Manchester: Manchester University Press.
______ 1965. "Reasonableness and Responsibility in the Law of Segmentary Societies." In *African Law: Adaptation and Development*, ed. Kuper, H., and L. Kuper. Berkeley: University of California Press.
______ 1969. *Ideas and Procedures in Customary Law*. London: Oxford University Press.
Grace, C., and P. Wilkinson. 1978. *Sociological Inquiry and Legal Phenomena*. London: Collier Macmillan.
Griffith, J. A. G. 1977. *The Politics of the Judiciary*. Glasgow: Fontana Press.
Grinnell, G. B. 1915. *The Fighting Cheyennes*. New York: Scribner's Sons.
Gulliver, P. H. 1969. "Case Studies of Law in Non-Western Societies." In *Law in Culture and Society*, ed. Nader, L. Chicago: Aldine Press.
Habermas, J. 1975. *Legitimation Crisis*. Boston: Beacon Press.
Hagerstrom, A. 1953. *Inquiries into the Nature of Law and Morals*, ed. Olivecrona K. Uppsala and Wiesbaden: Almquist & Wiksells.
Hall, G. D. G., ed. 1965., *The Treatise on the Laws and Customs of the Realm of England Commonly Called Glanvill*. London: Nelson.
Hamnett, I. 1977. Introduction to *Social Anthropology and Law*. A.S.A. Monograph no. 14. London: Academic Press.
Hansard Society, London. Great Britain. Parliament House of Lords. *The Parliamentary Debates (Hansard) Official Report*. London: H. M. Stationery Office.
Harari, A. 1962. *The Place of Negligence in the Law of Torts*. Sydney: Law Book Co. of Australasia.

Harris, J. W. 1980. *Legal Philosophies*. London: Butterworths.

Harrison, J. F. C. 1969. *Quest for the New Moral World: Robert Owen and the Owenites in Britain and America*. New York: Scribner's.

Hart, H. A. L. 1961. *The Concept of Law*. London: Oxford University Press.

Hayek, F. A. 1973. *Law, Legislation and Liberty*. Vol. 1, *Rules and Order*. London: Routledge & Kegan Paul.

Holmes, O. W. 1881. *The Common Law.*

Honoré, A. M. 1973. "Groups, Laws and Obedience." In *Oxford Essays in Jurisprudence*, 2d ser., ed. Simpson, A. W. B. London: Oxford University Press.

Hunt, A. 1978. *The Sociological Movement in Law*. London: Macmillan.

Jackson, R. M. 1967. *The Machinery of Justice in England*. 5th ed. Cambridge: Cambridge University Press.

James, J. S. 1974. *Stroud's Judicial Dictionary*. London: Sweet & Maxwell.

Kamenka, E., and E. A. Tay. 1975. "Beyond Bourgeois Individualism." In *Feudalism, Capitalism and Beyond*, ed. Kamenka, E., and R. S. Neale. Canberra: Australian National University Press.

Kibbutz Ha'artzi Movement. 1964. *Asuphot* (in Hebrew). Tel-Aviv: Kibbutz Ha'artzi.

Lawson, F. H. 1950. *Negligence in the Civil Law*. London: Oxford University Press.

Levi, E. 1970. *An Introduction to Legal Reasoning*. Chicago: University of Chicago Press.

Llewellyn, K. 1960. *The Common Law Tradition: Deciding Appeals*. Boston: Little, Brown.

Llewellyn, K., and E. A. Hoebel. *The Cheyenne Way*. Norman: University of Oklahoma Press.

Luhmann, N. 1977. *Funktion der Religion*. Frankfurt: Suhrkamp.

______ 1982. *The Differentiation of Society*. New York: Columbia University Press.

MacCormack, G. 1970. "Scandinavian Realism." *The Juridical Review*. The Law Journal of Scottish Universities 15, pt. 1, pp. 33–55.

MacGaffey, W. 1970. *Custom and Government in Lower Congo*. Berkeley: University of California Press.

Malinowski, B. 1926. *Crime and Custom in Savage Society*. London: Routledge & Kegan Paul.

Marx, K. 1955. "Critique of the Gotha Programme." In *Karl Marx and Frederick Engels, Selected Works*. Moscow: Foreign Languages Publishing House.

Merton, R. 1965. "Durkheim's Division of Labour in Society." In *Emile Durkheim*, ed. Nisbet, R. Englewood Cliffs, N.J.: Prentice-Hall.

Milsom, S. F. C. 1981. *Historical Foundations of the Common Law*. 2d ed. London: Butterworths.

Moore, S. F. 1978. *Law as Process*. London: Routledge & Kegan Paul.

Nadel, S. F. 1956. "Reason and Unreason in African Law." *Africa* 26: 160–73.

Olivecrona, K. 1959. "The Legal Theories of Axel Hagerstrom and Vilhelm Lundstedt." *Scandinavian Studies in Law* 3:125–156.

Overing, J., ed. 1985. *Reason and Morality*. A.S.A. Monograph no. 24, London: Tavistock.

Pashukanis, E. B. 1951. "General Theory of Law and Marxism." In *Soviet Legal Philosophy*, ed. Hazard, J. N. Cambridge: Harvard University Press.

Powell, R. 1957. *Current Legal Problems: The Unreasonableness of the Reasonable Man*. London: University College London, Stevens & Sons.

Radcliffe-Brown, A. R. 1952. *Structure and Function in Primitive Society*. Glencoe, Ill: Free Press.

Rattray, R. S. 1929. *Ashanti Law and Constitution*. Oxford: Oxford University Press.

Robson, P., and P. Watchman, eds. 1981. *Justice, Lord Denning and the Constitution*. Westmead: Gower.

Rosner, M., and N. Cohen. 1983. "Is Direct Democracy Feasible in Modern Society?" In *The Sociology of the Kibbutz: Studies of Israeli Society*, Vol. 3, ed. Krausz, E. New Brunswick, N.J.: Transaction.

Ross, A. 1946. *Towards a Realistic Jurisprudence: A Criticism of the Dualism in Law*. Copenhagen: Einar Munksgaard.

______ 1958. *On Law and Justice*. London: Stevens & Sons.

Saltman, M. 1977. *The Kipsigis: A Case Study in Changing Customary Law*. Cambridge: Schenkman.

______ 1981. "Legality and Ideology in the Kibbutz Movement." *International Journal of the Sociology of Law* 9:279–302.

______ 1985. "The Law Is a Ass: An Anthropological Appraisal." In *Reason and Morality*. A.S.A. Monograph no. 24, ed. Overing, J. London: Tavistock Press.

______ 1987. "Feudal Relationships and the Law: A Comparative Enquiry." *Comparative Studies in Society and History* 29:3.

Saltman, M., and H. Rosenfeld. 1990. "Rule of Law versus Political Interest: Contemporary Crises." *Law, Crime and Social Policy* 14(2).

Schmalenbach, H. 1961. "The Sociological Category of Communion." In *Theories of Society*, Vol. 1, Parsous, T. et al. (eds.). Glencoe, Ill.: Free Press.

Schmitthoff, C. M. 1979. "Lord Denning and the Contemporary Scene." *Journal of Business Law*. London: Stevens & Sons.

Schwartz, B., and H. W. R. Wade. 1972. *Legal Control of Government*. Oxford: Clarendon Press.

Schwartz, R., and J. Miller. 1964. "Legal Evolution and Societal Complexity." *American Journal of Sociology* 70:159–69.

Shapiro, A. E. 1976. "Law in the Kibbutz: A Reappraisal." *Law and Society Review* 10:415–42.

Shenker, B. 1986. *Intentional Communities*. London: Routledge & Kegan Paul.
Stone, J. 1964. *Legal System and Lawyers' Reasonings*. London: Stevens & Sons.
Thompson, E. P. 1978. *The Poverty of Theory and Other Essays*. New York and London: Monthly Review Press.
Twining, W. 1973. *Karl Llewellyn and the Realist Movement*. London: Weidenfeld & Nicolson.
Van de Berghe, P. L., and K. Peter. 1988. "Hutterites and Kibbutzniks: A Tale of Nepotistic Communism." *Man* 23(3):522–39.
Volosinov, V. N. 1985. "Verbal Interaction." In *Semiotics: An Introductory Anthology*, ed. Innis, R. E. Bloomington: Indiana University Press.
Wade, H. W. R. 1971. *Administrative Law*. 3d ed. Oxford: Clarendon Press.
Walker, D. W. 1980. *The Oxford Companion to Law*. Oxford: Oxford University Press.
Weisbrod, C. 1980. *The Boundaries of Utopia*. New York: Pantheon.
Young, E. 1981. "Developing a System? Lord Denning and Administrative Law." In *Justice, Lord Denning and the Constitution*, ed. Robson, P., and P. Watchman. Westmead: Gower.

Cases Cited

Associated Picture Houses Ltd. v. Wednesbury Corp. [1948] 1KB
Baltimore & Ohio Railroad Co. v. Goodman [1927] 275 U.S.
Becker v. Ministry of Defence [1970] PD238/70
Bravery v. Bravery [1954] P
British Railway Board v. Harrington [1972] AC
Chief Constable of Avon and Somerset v. Jones [1985] *Times Law Report* 13.11.1985
Commonwealth Smelting Ltd. and Another v. Guardian Royal Exchange Assurance Ltd. [1985] *Times Law Report* 5.12.1985
Davis v. Beason [1890] 133 U.S.
Davis v. Davis [1966] P
Glasgow Corporation v. Muir [1943] AC
Re Golay's Will Trusts, Morris v. Bridgewater and Others [1965] P
Horton v. London Graving Dock Co. Ltd. [1950] AC
Lanarkshire Steel Co. v. Caledonian Railway Co. [1903] SLR
Liversidge v. Anderson [1941] HL
Meron v. Ministry of Labour [1970] PD337,362-3/70
Mormon Church v. United States [1890] 136 U.S.
Newberry v. Cohen's (Smoked Salmon Ltd.) [1956] *Times Law Report* 27.4.1956
Perry v. Ellis [1946] SASR

R. v. Hillingdon London Borough Council *ex parte* Pulhofer and Another [1986] *Times Law Report* 7.2.1986
R. v. Secretary of State for Home Affairs *ex parte* Hosenball [1977] 1WLR 166
R. v. Sheffield Crown Court *ex parte* Brownlow [1980] 2 All ER
Reynolds v. United States [1878] 98 U.S.
Roberts v. Hopwood [1925] AC
Roy-Lewis v. Roy-Lewis [1954] P
Scott v. Scott [1951] P
Secretary of State v. Tameside Borough Council [1976] WLR
Shalit v. Ministry of Interior [1968] PD58/68
Stafford v. D.P.P. [1974] AC
State *ex rel.* Stephen Ball v. Anna Hand [1848] Western Law Journal
Ward v. Bradford Corporation [1972] 70 LGR
Woods v. Duncan [1946] AC

Index

For Product Safety Concerns and Information please contact our EU representative GPSR@taylorandfrancis.com
Taylor & Francis Verlag GmbH, Kaufingerstraße 24, 80331 München, Germany

www.ingramcontent.com/pod-product-compliance
Lightning Source LLC
LaVergne TN
LVHW021247011026
849160LV00010BA/936
* 9 7 8 1 4 1 2 8 5 5 9 1 4 *